TRADE AND DEVELOPMENT

Trade and Development

ESSAYS IN ECONOMICS

By V. K. RAMASWAMI

Sometime Chief Economic Adviser in the Indian Ministry of Finance

EDITED AND WITH AN INTRODUCTION BY
JAGDISH N. BHAGWATI
HARRY G. JOHNSON
T. N. SRINIVASAN

THE M.I.T. PRESS
Massachusetts Institute of Technology
Cambridge, Massachusetts

ISBN 0-262-18053-7

Library of Congress catalog card number: 72-1138

Printed in Great Britain
by Page Bros (Norwich) Ltd
Norwich, England

Contents

INTRODUCTION

by

JAGDISH N. BHAGWATI

HARRY G. JOHNSON

T. N. SRINIVASAN

V. K. Ramaswami died of carbon monoxide poisoning in New Delhi during the night of October 18th, 1969. This tragic accident prematurely ended a remarkable career which was marked by notable contributions to the theory of international economics and the conduct of Indian economic policy.

Ramaswami was born in 1929 and spent much of his childhood in the city of Baroda in Western India, now in the State of Gujarat. Baroda State was then outside British India, and Ramaswami's father, V. T. Krishnamachari, was the Diwan (Prime Minister) to the Maharaja of Baroda. The Baroda court was distinguished for its patronage of great musicians and Ramaswami liked to recall how he had learnt classical music from Ustad Faiyaz Khan, India's leading musician, until his 'voice broke'!

Ramaswami later went to Madras, the State to which his family originally belonged, to graduate from Madras University, with First Class Honours in Economics. He left in 1947 for Balliol College, Oxford, to study Politics, Philosophy and Economics. His career there was uniformly brilliant, culminating in a First, the Webb–Medley Scholarship and a Junior Research Fellowship at Balliol. Oxford suited his shy and gentle temperament, and he was to return to it from time to time in his later years.

On returning home, Ramaswami joined the Reserve Bank of India (India's central bank) as a member of its economic research staff. This was to be the beginning of a distinguished career which took him right to the top of the economics bureaucracy as the Chief Economic Adviser in the Ministry of Finance. *En route* there, he was to spend many years as the Economic Adviser to the Ministries in charge of Industrial Development and (foreign) Commerce: these were his intellectually formative years, and he was often to return to the problems of commercial policy in his academic endeavours. As Chief Economic Adviser in the Ministry of Finance, Ramaswami had been put into the position of having to oversee the entire range of economic policies of the Indian government: and to this task he brought much enthusiasm, total commitment and an acuteness of mind which, even in the distinguished civil service of India, was quite unusual and widely admired.

It is quite remarkable that, in addition to these numerous governmental functions to which he gave his closest and most dedicated attention, Ramaswami managed to find the time to pursue his academic and research interests in economics to the extent that he left a significant impact on the theory of international trade. He worked on his theoretical papers in the late evenings and early mornings, having often had an exhausting and gruelling day full of meetings at the Ministry of Finance: his intellectual curiosity and tenacity were extraordinary. But he also escaped abroad occasionally, for longer periods of quiet and undisturbed research. He was at Balliol College, Oxford, in 1957–8 and at the MIT Centre for International Studies during 1967–8. He produced a number of papers during these visits; and he was to be remembered there not only for his impressive analytical abilities but also for the generosity of his temperament.

The range of his theoretical output was wide, as is indeed clear from the collection of his more important papers in this volume. It ranged from the theory of trade and growth, on which he wrote early in his career, to the theory of optimal policy intervention in the presence of distortions and the theory of effective protection.

A number of these papers had their origins in the practical problems with which Ramaswami was occupied. For example, when he was concerned with import entitlement schemes for export promotion, he became interested in the theory of trade in intermediate goods, which led him eventually to work in the area of effective protection and on the problem of devising optimal trade policies to collect a given total revenue when some factors are imported. Similarly, his interest in the theory of optimal policy in the presence of domestic distortions was in response to his preoccupations with tariffs and quantitative restrictions in the context of Indian economic policies. This interaction of policy and theory, which both startled the bureaucratic economists with the subtlety of his economic logic and insights and produced significant theorems in international economic analysis with policy relevance, was one of the most remarkable aspects of Ramaswami's work.

At the same time, like most theorists, Ramaswami pursued economic ideas for their intrinsic interest. He was, for example, early in noticing (when he was visiting Balliol in 1957–8) that the factor price equalization theorem did not necessarily imply interest rate equalization. This showed great insight and led eventually to Paul Samuelson's major paper on the equalization of interest rates in the Haberler *Festschrift*. Yet another significant contribution made by Ramaswami, during his stay at Oxford, was the introduction of a capital goods sector into the Johnson–Corden type of trade-and-growth model which previously had been developed in the framework of the traditional model of two domestic primary factors producing two traded consumer goods.

Among Ramaswami's major analytical contributions to trade theory must be counted his work on optimal policy intervention in the presence of distortion and on the theory of trade in intermediate goods. Around 1962, Ramaswami became interested in the question of whether tariff policy was the optimal policy in the presence of *domestic* distortions. While it had been recognized that the optimal policy in the presence of monopoly power in trade (which is a *foreign* distortion) is a tariff, it was not clearly realized until the 1963 (joint) paper of Ramaswami and Bhagwati that the same theory implied that, for a *domestic* distortion, a domestic policy instrument is called for.

Thus, for the case of a Meade-type production externality, it was generally considered that a tariff and a production tax-cum-subsidy could not be ranked *vis-à-vis* each other on purely economic grounds. Hence the infant-industry argument was agreed to be an exception to the free-trade case but whether protection should be provided by subsidy or tariffs was considered to be a question to be decided on political and administrative grounds; and Marshall and Taussig opted against tariffs in light of the disillusioning experience with tariff making. Ramaswami's work cut through this difficulty and showed that, for a production externality, the production tax-cum-subsidy policy and *not a tariff policy* was optimal.

This paper drastically reduced the theoretical role of tariffs as a policy instrument. Tariffs were seen now to be the optimal, *first-best* policy *only* when there was monopoly power in trade and domestic policies such as production, consumption, and factor-use tax-cum-subsidies were seen to be the correct optimal policies when the distortions were in the production, consumption and factor markets respectively.

This paper also investigated *second-best* policies: if a production tax-cum-subsidy could not be used for correcting a production externality, could a tariff then be used to *improve* welfare? Here, the paper argued that there may not exist a tariff that will improve welfare. This was a stronger proposition which consigned tariff protection to a still inferior position: not merely were tariffs not the optimal policies for domestic distortions but they might not even be *welfare-improving* policies.

This latter proposition, however, was shown by Kemp and Negishi to be false. They demonstrated that, in general, a (suitably chosen) tariff policy will improve welfare in the presence of domestic (production) distortions; and also that a (suitably chosen) production tax-cum-subsidy policy will improve welfare in the presence of a foreign distortion (i.e. when there is monopoly power in trade). This prompted Ramaswami, in turn (with Bhagwati and Srinivasan) to extend the analysis to the ranking of *all* policy instruments; production, consumption and factor-use tax-cum-subsidies as well as trade taxes. This analysis was to complete the logical analysis of the question of ranking alternative policies in the presence of different distortions.

Another significant contribution of Ramaswami's was in the field of trade in intermediate goods. He was drawn to Max Corden's excellent statement of the theory of effective-protective rates (EPR) in the *Journal of Political Economy* (1966) largely because of the interest that he had developed in questions of optimal trade policy when some factors of production were traded. With his usual analytical acumen, however, he realized that the EPR theory had to be checked out in the framework of a general equilibrium model.

Thus, independently of two other researchers in this area abroad (Tan and Ruffin), Ramaswami proceeded to develop (along with Srinivasan) a general equilibrium analysis of the problem as to whether the EPR theory furnished an adequate basis for ranking activities by an index which would predict correctly the resource-allocational effects *vis-à-vis* the free trade situation. This important paper demonstrated how, in the *general* case of substitution between imported and domestic factors, it was *impossible* to construct an EPR index which would predict accurately the required resource-allocational effects. Later, a restrictive sufficient restriction on the nature of substitution was to be introduced by Corden, and a new 'value-added-product' definition of EPR devised by him, to indicate how the Ramaswami-Srinivasan 'impossibility theorem' could be skirted around. In addition to Corden's later work, this paper of Ramaswami's was to stimulate important new work in this area by Ronald Jones and other trade theorists.

The other important (joint) paper of Ramaswami dealt with the problem of devising an optimal *trade* tax to collect pre-assigned revenue. This paper is a significant contribution to the theory of public finance and furnished theoretical support to the widespread policy of giving exemption from trade taxes to intermediates used in export production.

While the bulk of Ramaswami's work was in the field of international trade, he had begun to move into other areas as well towards the end of his life. His *Oxford Economic Papers* article on two-sector growth models is a remarkable piece of exposition and synthesis, bringing together a vast amount of esoteric, mathematical literature and rendering it accessible to mathematically unsophisticated economists. Coming from a theorist without high mathematical expertise, this is quite a *tour de force*. And its geometrical techniques, which were invented with great originality, have also been used with efficacy by other theorists such as Harry Johnson.

At the time of his death, Ramaswami was engaged in yet newer areas of research: he left behind a number of unfinished manuscripts and a near-finished manuscript on monetary theory. The great spurt in his theoretical output and the widening of his intellectual interests towards the end of his life add a particular element of tragedy to his sudden death.

Ramaswami was remarkable, however, not merely for his intellectual distinction and scholarly achievements; he also had unique personal qualities. He reached out easily beyond himself to give his energies and empathy to deserving objectives and causes. The economists in India, and not merely in Delhi where Ramaswami worked and lived, were witnesses to his unstinting assistance in building up the universities and research institutes. And he combined these concerns about the growth of great centres of economic research in India with a broad, international outlook and indentification with the world community of scholars which made him feel intellectually and emotionally at home wherever he went.

Above all, however, his friends will recall the unforgettable warmth and affection that he could bring to his close friendships and his capacity to give invariably more than he received. For these rare qualities, as much as for his many contributions to the theory of international trade, he will be remembered.*

August 1970

---

*In view of these remarkable achievements and qualities, it was natural that Ramaswami's death should be recorded in obituary notices both in India and abroad. The obituaries in *The Indian Economic Review* and *The Journal of Political Economy* among whose editors Ramaswami had close personal friends and intellectual colleagues, contain in their own way many of the sentiments and the evaluations of Ramaswami's intellectual attainments that we have expressed here.

1. Domestic Distortions, Tariffs, and the Theory of Optimum Subsidy[*][1]

There is confusion of varying degrees in the current literature on trade theory concerning the desirable form of intervention in foreign trade when the economy is characterized by domestic distortions (divergences of the commodity price ratios from the corresponding marginal rates of transformation). For instance, the age-old debate over whether tariffs or subsidies should be used to protect an infant industry is still carried on in terms of the respective political and psychological merits of the two forms of protection while their relative economic advantages are assumed not to point in the direction of a definite choice.[2]

Three questions about the use of tariffs when domestic distortions exist need to be distinguished here. (1) Is a tariff necessarily superior to free trade (that is, can a tariff rate always be found that yields a welfare position superior to that produced by free trade)? (2) Is a tariff policy necessarily superior to any other form of *trade* policy? (3) If the choice can be made from the entire range of policy instruments, which is the optimal economic policy?

In Section I we state the general theory that provides the answers to these three questions. In the light of this theory, we examine the

[*]*Journal of Political Economy*, Vol. LXXI, No. 1, February 1963, pp. 44–50.
[1] An early draft of this paper was read to seminars at Massachusetts Institute of Technology, the University of Chicago, and Stanford University by one of the authors. C. P. Kindleberger and H. G. Johnson have made useful suggestions.

[2] For instance, C. P. Kindleberger in his *International Economics*, Homewood, Ill.; Richard D. Irwin, Inc., 1958, as does also G. Haberler in his *Theory of International Trade*, Edinburgh: William Hodge & Co., 1936, states the economic argument in favour of subsidies and tariffs without stating definitely that one is invariably superior to the other from the economic viewpoint.
[3] G. Haberler, 'Some Problems in the Pure Theory of International Trade', *Economic Journal*, Vol. LX, June 1950, pp. 223–40.

propositions advanced in the two central contributions to trade theory in this field: Haberler's justly celebrated 1950 *Economic Journal* paper[3] and Hagen's recent analysis of wage differentials.[1] Section II examines these two analyses and section III concludes with some observations concerning the relative advantages of tariffs and subsidies from the practical viewpoint.

I. GENERAL THEORY

The three questions posed here can be effectively answered by analysing the characteristics of an optimum solution. Thus, for instance, the optimum tariff argument can be stated elegantly in terms of these characteristics. The achievement of an optimum solution is characterized (assuming an interior maximum) by the equality of the foreign rate of transformation (FRT), the domestic rate of transformation in production (DRT), and the domestic rate of substitution in consumption (DRS). If the country has monopoly power in trade, a competitive free trade solution will be characterized by $DRS = DRT \neq FRT$. By introducing a suitable tariff, a country can achieve $DRS = DRT = FRT$. A subsidy (tax) on the domestic production of importables (exportables) could equalize DRT and FRT but would destroy the equality of DRS with DRT. Hence it is clear that a tax-cum-subsidy on domestic production is necessarily inferior to an optimum tariff. Moreover it may be impossible in any given empirical situation to devise a tax-cum-subsidy that would yield a solution superior to that arrived at under free trade.

By analogy we can argue that, in the case of domestic distortions, $DRS = FRT \neq DRT$ under free trade. A suitable tariff can equalize FRT and DRT but would destroy the equality between DRS and FRT. Hence it is clear that no tariff may exist that would yield a solution superior to that under free trade. A suitable tax-cum-subsidy on domestic production, however, would enable the policy-maker to secure $DRS = FRT = DRT$ and hence is necessarily the optimum solution. Hence a tariff policy is also necessarily inferior to an optimum tax-cum-subsidy policy. And the same argument must hold true of trade subsidies as well since they also, like tariffs, are directed at *foreign* trade whereas the problem to be tackled is one of *domestic* distortion.

[1] E. Hagen, 'An Economic Justification of Protectionism', *Quarterly Journal of Economics*, Vol. LXXII, November 1958, pp. 496–514.

Three propositions, therefore, follow in the case of domestic distortions. (1) A tariff is not necessarily superior to free trade. (2) A tariff is not necessarily superior to an export (or import) subsidy. (3) A policy permitting the attainment of maximum welfare involves a tax-cum-subsidy on domestic production. Just as there exists an optimum tariff policy for a divergence between foreign prices and *FRT*, so there exists an *optimum subsidy* (or an equivalent tax-cum-subsidy) policy for a divergence between domestic prices and *DRT*.

II. HABERLER ON EXTERNAL ECONOMIES

A divergence between the domestic commodity price ratios and the marginal rates of transformation between commodities may arise from what are usually described as 'external economies'. These may take various forms.[1] It is most fashionable at the moment to discuss the external economies arising from the interdependence of investment decisions.[2]

Haberler analyses this problem in terms of the standard two-good, two-factor model of trade theory, using geometrical methods. Haberler is aware that a tariff is not necessarily superior to free trade. However, he is in error concerning the relative advantages of tariffs and trade subsidies. Further, he does not discuss the optimum economic policy under the circumstances.

Haberler distinguishes between two situations according to whether the domestic production of importables rises or falls (what he calls the direction of 'specialization'). We shall analyse each case separately.

Case 1

In the former case, illustrated here in Figure 1a, *AB* is the

[1] According to Haberler, 'there may be a deviation between social and private cost due to external economies or diseconomies, i.e. due to certain cost-raising or cost-reduction factors which would come into play if one industry expanded and the other contracted—factors which for some reason or other are not, or not sufficiently, allowed for in private cost calculations' ('Some Problems . . .', *op cit.*, p. 236).

[2] This has been analysed in the context of international trade by J. Bhagwati, 'The Theory of Comparative Advantage in the Context of Under-development and Growth', *Pakistan Development Review*, Vol. II, No. 3, Autumn 1962, pp. 339–53. See also H. Chenery, 'The Interdependence of Investment Decisions', in Moses Abramovitz *et al.*, *The Allocation of Economic Resources*, Stanford, Calif., Stanford University Press, 1959.

B

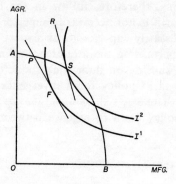

FIGURE 1a

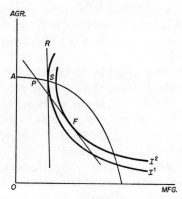

FIGURE 1b

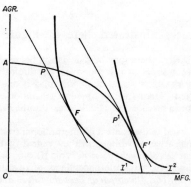

FIGURE 1c

production possibility curve. The discrepancy between the domestic price ratio and the domestic rate of transformation (*DRT*) leads to self-sufficiency equilibrium at *S*. Free trade, at the *given* international price *PF*, leads to production at *P*, consumption at *F*, export of agricultural goods, and a deterioration in welfare.[1]

The following comments are warranted. First, although Haberler does not state this explicitly, it can be shown that prohibitive protection may make the country worse off (Figure 1b). Second, it follows from Section I that *no* tariff may be superior to free trade (this is implicit, we think, in Haberler's statements elsewhere in his paper). Finally, the optimum result could be achieved by a policy of tax-cum-subsidy on domestic production. Such a policy is illustrated in Figure 1c where the tax-cum-subsidy eliminates the divergence between commodity prices and *DRT* and brings production to *P'* and consumption to *F'*.

Case 2

Haberler distinguishes the other case by arguing that the self-sufficiency price ratio *RS* may be less steep than the *given* foreign price ratio *PF*. Here the production point is shifted to the right by free trade.[2] In this case, Haberler argues that 'the country would specialize in the 'right' direction but not sufficiently. *It would after trade be better off than before, but it would not reach the optimum point . . . In that case an export or import subsidy (rather than a tariff) would be indicated.*[3]

While Haberler is right in arguing that a movement to the right of *S*, when free trade is introduced, will necessarily be beneficial, his conclusion that an export (or import) subsidy is indicated and would be preferable to a tariff is erroneous in every rigorous sense in which it may be understood. First, it cannot be argued that the optimal solution when the policy used is an export (or import) subsidy will be necessarily superior to that when the policy used is a tariff. As

[1] Haberler wrongly seems to imply that the country must export agricultural goods in this case. There is no reason, *once there is a domestic distortion*, why a country should necessarily export the commodity that is cheaper than abroad in the absence of trade.

[2] This, of course, is erroneous, as noted in n.3 p. 236 Haberler implies that under free trade manufactures will now become the exported good. Haberler also describes this case as characterized by specialization in the 'right' direction. He is right if, by this, he means that the movement of the production point to the right of *S*, caused by free trade, will necessarily improve welfare. He is wrong, however, if he means that the commodity exported will be that which would have been exported if the divergence did not exist.

[3] Haberler, 'Some Problems . . .', *op cit.*, p. 237. Our italics.

argued in Section I, both policies are handicapped as they seek to affect *foreign* trade whereas the distortion is *domestic*; there is no reason why one should necessarily be better than the other. Second, nor can one maintain that an export (or import) subsidy will necessarily exist that will be superior to free trade, just as one cannot maintain that a tariff necessarily will be available that is superior to free trade. Third, the optimum solution again is to impose a tax-cum-subsidy on domestic production.

Case 3

Hagen on Wage Differentials. A divergence between *DRT* and the domestic price ratio, arising from factor-market imperfections in the form of intersectoral wage differentials, has been discussed in relation to trade policy by Hagen. Before we proceed to Hagen's analysis, certain observations concerning the circumstances in which differential remuneration causes a distortion are in order.

The observed wage differentials between the urban and rural sector may *not* represent a genuine distortion. For instance, they may reflect (1) a utility preference between occupations on the part of the wage-earners, or (2) a rent (on scarce skills), or (3) a return on investment in human capital (by training), or (4) a return on investment in the cost of movement (from the rural to the urban sector). There *would* be a distortion, however, where the differential is attributable to (5) trade-union intervention, or (6) prestige-cum-humanitarian grounds ('I must pay my man a decent wage') that fix wages at varying levels in different sectors. Two other types of explanations may also be discussed: (7) Hagen argues that the differential occurs in manufacture because this is the advancing sector and growing activities inevitably have to pay higher wages to draw labour away from other industries. While this 'dynamic' argument appears to provide support for the distortionary character of the differential, there are difficulties with it. For instance, the fact that a differential has to be maintained to draw labour away may very well be due to the cost of movement.[1] (8) A more substantive argument is that the rural sector affords employment to non-adult members of the family whereas, in the urban sector, the adult alone gets employment (owing to institutional reasons such as factory acts). Hence, to migrate, an adult would need to be compensated for the loss of

---

[1] Other difficulties also arise when the argument is used in conjunction with a static analysis. These will be discussed later.

employment by the non-adult members of his family.[1] If this is the case, there is certainly a market imperfection (assuming that individual preferences rather than collective preferences, expressed in legislation, are relevant) and hence distortion.[2]

In the following analysis, we shall assume that the wage differential represents a genuine distortion while remaining sceptical about the degree to which such distortions obtain in the actual world.[3] We will also adopt Hagen's analytical framework of a two-commodity, two-factor model and a *constant* wage differential. The assumption of constancy of the wage differential raises some difficulties, probably with reasons (3) and (6) but certainly with reason (7), on which Hagen mainly relies. As will be seen presently, Hagen's analysis involves the *contraction* of manufactures after the introduction of trade; if the wage differential is due to the fact that manufactures are expanding and drawing labour away, it should surely reverse itself during the transition from autarchy to free trade. The difficulty is that Hagen, in relying upon reason (7) while using traditional trade analysis, is illegitimately superimposing a dynamic argument upon a comparative statics framework. To analyse the distortion arising from reason (8) one needs an explicitly dynamic analysis. Hence, the following analysis applies, strictly speaking, only to distortions produced by reasons (5) and (6).

Hagen concludes that a tariff is superior to free trade when the *importable manufacturing* activity has to pay the higher wage.

> As a result of the wage disparity, manufacturing industry will be undersold by imports when the foreign exchanges are in equilibrium. Protection which permits such industry to exist will increase real income in the economy. However, a subsidy per unit of labour equal to the wage differential will increase real income further, and if

---

[1] This hypothesis was suggested to us by D. Mazumdar.

[2] This 'distortion', unlike the others, involves a contraction of the labour force as labour moves from one sector to another. Hence, the following analysis does not apply and a fresh solution, incorporating a changing labour supply, is called for. Note here also that the wage differential variety of distortion is quite distinct from the distortion caused when, although the wage is identical between sectors, it differs from the 'shadow' optimal wage. This distinction has been blurred by recent analysts, especially W. A. Lewis, 'Economic Development with Unlimited Supplies of Labor', *Manchester School*, Vol. XXII, May 1959, and H. Myint, 'Infant Industry Arguments for Assistance to Industries in the Setting of Dynamic Trade Theory' (paper presented to a conference on 'Trade in a Developing World', International Economic Association, September 1961). Also see Bhagwati, *op cit.*

[3] A. Kafka, 'A New Argument for Protectionism', *Quarterly Journal of Economics*, Vol. LXXVI, February 1962, pp. 163–6.

combined with free trade will permit attaining an *optimum optimorum*.[1]

Hagen works successively with two models that differ only in the assumption concerning the number of factors of production. Since the first model has only one factor and is only a special case of the second, two-factor model, we shall concentrate here on the latter. It is assumed that all the standard Paretian conditions obtain except for the wage differential. We begin with Hagen's analysis and then comment on it.

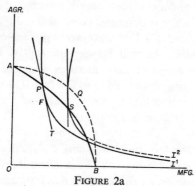

FIGURE 2a

In Figure 2a, AQB is the production possibility curve on the assumption of a wage uniform between the two sectors. APB is the production possibility curve, assuming the given wage differential.[2] The wage differential against manufactures, aside from reducing

[1] *Op cit.*, p. 498. Hagen himself does not state explicitly that he is confining the analysis to the case where the differential operates against the importable activity. If the differential were to work in the contrary direction, the results would naturally have to be modified radically.

[2] The reader can satisfy himself as to the 'shrinking in' of the production possibility curve by manipulating the Edgeworth box diagram. The careful reader of Hagen's paper will note that Hagen draws the 'shrunk-in' production possibility curve so that it is convex (in the mathematical sense). This, however, is a property that does not necessarily follow from the assumptions made, and it is possible to produce counter-examples of concavity, although we have not been able to produce a general mathematical proof. (When this paper was read at Stanford, Paul David drew attention to A. Fishlow and P. David's 'Optimal Resource Allocation in an Imperfect Market Setting', *Journal of Political Economy*, Vol. LXIX, December 1961, pp. 529–46, for a proof of this proposition. These writers have also anticipated our criticism concerning Hagen's confusion of statics and dynamics.) We shall use the convex curve, however, as it enables us to state our propositions in terms of equalities and without bothering about second-order conditions; the substance of the propositions *that interest us here* is unaffected by this complication. The divergence between the commodity price ratio and the domestic rate of transformation, which also results from the wage differential, needs a rigorous proof, which can be found by the reader in Hagen, *op. cit.*, pp. 507–8.

the production feasibilities, will make the commodity price ratio, at any production point on *APB*, steeper than the rate of transformation along *APB* so that the price ratio understates the profitability of transforming agriculture into manufactures. *PT* being the foreign price ratio, the economy produces at *P* and consumes at *F* under free trade. Under self-sufficiency, however, the relative price of manufactures being higher, the economy would produce and consume at *S* and be better off. From this, Hagen concludes: 'Protection of manufacturing from foreign trade will increase real income.[1]

However, the conclusion must be rectified. First, as illustrated in Figure 2b, where the contrary possibility is shown, prohibitive pro-

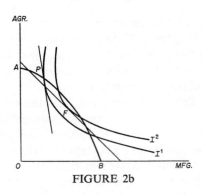

FIGURE 2b

tection is not necessarily superior to free trade. Second, it may further be impossible, as argued in Section I, to find any level of tariff (or trade subsidy) that is superior to free trade. Third, a tax-cum-subsidy on the domestic production of the commodities, which eliminates the divergence between the price ratio and *DRT* (along *APB*) would necessarily yield a better solution than protection. In Figure 2c, *F'* represents the consumption and *P'* the production reached by the pursuit of such a tax-cum-subsidy policy.[2]

---

[1] Hagen, *op. cit.*, p. 510.
[2] In relation to this point, it is also worth noting that the standard procedure adopted by several tariff commissions, of choosing a tariff rate that just offsets the differential between the average domestic cost at some *arbitrary*, given production of the existing units and the landed (c.i.f.) cost, is not necessarily correct. There is no reason why the tariff rate which just offsets this differential is necessarily the tariff rate which is optimum from the viewpoint of economic policy.

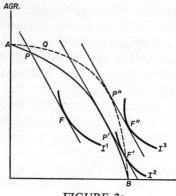

FIGURE 2c

Finally, a policy of tax-cum-subsidy on labour use would achieve equilibrium production at P'' and consumption at F'' in Figure 2c and produce the 'first-best" result, as recognized by Hagen.

Note that, in contrast to the case of external economies, the optimum tax-cum-subsidy on domestic production, while superior to protection or trade subsidy, does not yield the *optimum optimorum* in the wage-differential case. The reason is straightforward. The wage differential causes *not merely* a domestic distortion but *also* a restriction of the production possibility curve. A tax-cum-subsidy on domestic production measure will, therefore, merely eliminate the domestic distortion but not restore the economy to the Paretian production possibility curve (AQB). It will thus achieve the equality of *FRT* and *DRS* with *DRT* along *the restricted production possibility curve* (APB) and hence constitute the optimal solution when the wage differential cannot be directly eliminated. Where, however, a direct attack on the wage differential is permitted, the fully optimal, 'first-best' solution can be achieved by a policy of tax-cum-subsidy on factor use.

III. CONCLUSION

We have argued here that an optimum subsidy (or a tax-cum-subsidy equivalent) is necessarily superior to any tariff when the distortion is domestic. It may be questioned, however, whether this advantage would obtain in practice. This question, of course, cannot be settled purely at the economic level. A fully satisfactory treatment of this issue would necessarily involve discipline ranging from politics to psychology. However, by way of conclusion, we think it would be useful to consider a few arguments that are relevant to the final, realistic choice of policy.

1. The contention that the payment of subsidies would involve the collection of taxes which in practice cannot be levied in a non-distortionary fashion is fallacious. A tax-cum-subsidy scheme could always be devised that would *both* eliminate the estimated divergence and collect taxes sufficient to pay the subsidies.

2. The estimation problem is also easier with subsidies than with tariffs. The former involves estimating merely the divergence between the commodity price ratio and *DRT* (at the relevant production point). The latter must extend the exercises necessarily to the estimation of the relevant *DRS* (which involves locating both the right level of income *and* the relevant consumption point).

3. The political argument has usually been claimed by free traders to favour the payment of subsidies under external economy arguments like infant industries. It is thought that it would be difficult to pay a subsidy longer than strictly necessary whereas a tariff may be more difficult to abolish. It must be pointed out, however, that this argument also pulls the other way because, precisely for the reasons which make a subsidy difficult to continue, a subsidy is difficult to choose in preference to a tariff.

2. Domestic Distortions, Tariffs, and the Theory of Optimum Subsidy: Some Further Results[1]

Bhagwati and Ramaswami [1] showed that if there is a distortion, the Paretian first-best policy is to intervene with a tax (subsidy) at the point at which the distortion occurs. Hence a domestic tax-cum-subsidy with respect to production would be first-best optimal when there was a *domestic* distortion (defined as the divergence between domestic prices and the marginal rate of transformation in domestic production) just as a tariff policy would be first-best optimal under monopoly power in trade (which involves a *foreign* distortion). An important corollary, for the case of a distortionary wage differential, is that while a tax-cum-subsidy policy with respect to factor use would be first-best optimal, the second-best optimal policy would be a *domestic* production tax-cum-subsidy rather than a tariff policy.

While these central results are valid, Kemp and Negishi [2] have correctly argued that two subsidiary propositions of Bhagwati and Ramaswami [1] are false. These are (1) that no tariff (export subsidy) may exist which is superior to free trade in the presence of a domestic distortion, and (2) that no production tax-cum-subsidy may yield greater welfare than non-intervention when the nation has monopoly power.

We can demonstrate, however, that the Kemp–Negishi results are, in fact, special cases of the first of the following two theorems in the theory of second-best, which we shall prove:

Theorem 1. If under laissez-faire two of the variables *DRS*, *DRT*, and *FRT* are equal while the third has a different value, and the

---

[1] H. G. Johnson has provided useful comments on an earlier draft of this note.

24

policy measure that will secure equal values of the three variables cannot be applied, some policy measure exists that will raise welfare above the laisse-faire level, though it will destroy the equality of the first two variables.[1]

Theorem 2. If under laissez-faire all three variables *DRS*, *DRT* and *FRT* have different values, and both of the policy measures that will secure equal values of the three variables cannot be applied, no feasible form of intervention may exist that will raise welfare.

We use the following notation:

C_i, X_i denote the consumption and domestic output, respectively of commodity i, $i = 1, 2$.

p_c denotes the ratio of the price of the first to that of the second commodity confronting consumers (*DRS*).

p_t denotes $DRT = - dX_2/dX_1$.

p_f denotes the ratio of the world price of the first commodity to that of the second commodity, that is, the *average* terms of trade. The marginal terms of trade $FRT = p_f$ only in the special case in which national monopoly power does not exist.

The welfare function $U(C_1, C_2)$ and the production functions are assumed to be differentiable as required. The U_i denotes the marginal utility of commodity i ($i = 1, 2$). It is assumed throughout the analysis that under laissez-faire there is non-specialization in consumption and production, and that some trade takes place.

Our procedure is as follows. We derive the expression for the change in welfare when there is a slight movement away from an initial equilibrium in which there is no intervention. If the levy of some tax (subsidy) at a *small* rate will secure a positive value for this expression, we can conclude that welfare can be raised above the laissez-faire level by applying this tax (subsidy). Note that in such a case some *finite* (and not merely infinitesimal) tax (subsidy) rate will exist which yields greater welfare than laissez-faire. If the derivative of welfare with respect to the rate of some tax (subsidy) is non-zero at the laissez-faire point, then by continuity it is non-zero for some finite interval of values of the tax (subsidy) rate around the laissez-faire

---

[1] *DRS*, *DRT* and *FRT* denote, respectively, the marginal domestic rate of substitution in consumption, the marginal domestic rate of transformation in production, and the marginal rate of transformation through trade.

point. If, on the other hand, the levy of some tax (subsidy) at a small rate does not change welfare, then there may not exist any rate of this tax (subsidy) which secures more welfare than under non-intervention.[1]

The change in welfare due to a small deviation from an initial laissez-faire equilibrium is

$$dU = U_1 dC_1 + U_2 dC_2 = U_2 \left(\frac{U_1}{U_2} dC_1 + dC_2 \right).$$

The marginal condition for utility maximization is that $U_1/U_2 = p_c$. So,

$$dU = U_2(p_c dC_1 + dC_2) = U_2[p_f dC_1 + dC_2 + (p_c - p_f)dC_1]$$
$$= U_2[d(p_f C_1 + C_2) - C_1 dp_f + (p_c - p_f)dC_1].$$

Assuming balanced trade, $p_f C_1 + C_2 = p_f X_1 + X_2$. So,

$$dU = U_2[d(p_f X_1 + X_2) - C_1 dp_f + (p_c - p_f)dC_1]$$
$$= U_2[p_f dX_1 + dX_2 + (X_1 - C_1)dp_f + (p_c - p_f)dC_1]$$
$$= U_2 \left[dX_1 \left(p_f + \frac{dX_2}{dX_1} \right) + (X_1 - C_1)dp_f + (p_c - p_f)dC_1 \right]$$
$$= U_2[dX_1(p_f - p_t) + (X_1 - C_1)dp_f + (p_c - p_f)dC_1]. \quad \ldots \quad (1)$$

Theorem 1

There are three ways in which, under laissez-faire, two of the variables *DRS*, *DRT* and *FRT* have equal values, while the third has a different value: $DRS = FRT \neq DRT$, $DRS = DRT \neq FRT$, and $DRS \neq DRT = FRT$. We consider these three cases in turn.

Case 1. Assume that national monopoly power does not exist. We then discuss two alternative cases in turn: (1) production externality,[2] and (2) wage differential in one activity.[3] In either case, *DRS* =

---

[1] If the function relating the level of welfare and the rate of a specified tax (subsidy) is concave and has a local maximum at the laissez-faire point, then this local maximum *must* be a global maximum, and a finite tax (subsidy) *must* reduce welfare below the laissez-faire level. If this function is not concave, however, the local maximum need not be a global maximum and therefore some finite tax (subsidy) *may* exist which raises welfare above the laissez-faire level.

[2] A production externality that would produce a domestic distortion, in the sense of a divergence between the domestic prices and *DRT*, is where the production functions are the following: $X = X(Lx, Kx)$; $Y = Y(Ly, Ky, X)$, where the output of commodity y is a function of not merely the inputs of labour (Ly) and capital (Ky) but also the output level of commodity x, but the market does not remunerate the x-producers for this productivity.

[3] We will be assuming that the wage differential is distortionary, as in Bhagwati and Ramaswami [1].

$FRT \neq DRT$, and we have $p_c = p_f$, $dp_f = 0$ and $p_f \neq p_t$. So equation (1) reduces to:

$$dU = U_2[dX_1(p_f - p_t)]. \ldots \ldots \ldots \ldots (2)$$

It is clear that any policy measure that slightly increases (reduces) the output of the first commodity will raise welfare, if p_f is greater (less) than p_t.

So if, in the externality case, it is not feasible to secure first-best through the levy of a production tax-cum-subsidy, greater welfare than under laissez-faire can be obtained if (1) a tariff (trade subsidy) or (2) a factor tax-cum-subsidy is imposed. Note further that a tariff is *not* necessarily superior to a factor tax-cum-subsidy policy. Which of these measures is preferable in a given situation will depend on the form of the welfare and production functions. Thus, in any specific situation, a factor tax-cum-subsidy policy may be the second-best optimal policy, and the tariff (trade subsidy) the *third-best* optimal policy.[1]

In the case of a distortionary wage differential, the first-best policy is a factor tax-cum-subsidy, the second-best policy is a production tax-cum-subsidy, and the third-best policy is the tariff.[2]

Case 2. Now assume that there is no domestic distortion but national monopoly power exists, so that $DRS = DRT \neq FRT$ under laissez-faire. Then $p_c = p_t = p_f$ and $dp_f \neq 0$; so equation (1) reduces to

$$dU = U_2(X_1 - C_1)dp_f. \ldots \ldots \ldots \ldots (3)$$

Thus production, consumption, and factor-use tax-cum-subsidies will exist that will raise welfare above the laissez-faire level by changing the marginal rate of transformation through trade. It would appear, however, that we cannot determine *a priori* what the second-best, optimal policy will be; and the ranking of the three policies—production, consumption and factor-use tax-cum-subsidies —which are available when the first-best tariff policy is ruled out, will depend on the specific situation being considered.

[1] Thus Kemp and Negishi [2] who do not consider the entire range of policies that may be available when the first-best policy is ruled out, imply incorrectly that the 'second-best, optimal' policy in a situation with domestic distortions will be a tariff (trade subsidy) policy.

[2] Note that a finite consumption tax-cum-subsidy policy can only hurt the economy by adding a consumption loss to the loss already being suffered by the economy, thanks to the distortion.

Case 3. Suppose now that there is no national monopoly power, or distortion, or externality in production but that the sellers of one commodity charge consumers a uniform premium over the cost of both domestic and imported supplies. Then, under laissez-faire, $DRS \neq DRT = FRT$. We have $dp_f = 0$, $p_f = p_t$, $p_c \neq p_f$; so equation (1) reduces to

$$dU = U_2[p_c - p_f)dC_1]. \quad \dots \dots \dots \dots (4)$$

Thus, clearly the levy of a consumption tax-cum-subsidy will secure Paretian first-best, Furthermore, levy of tariff is necessarily superior to laissez-faire. Moreover, the imposition of production or factor-use taxes (subsidies) *may* also be superior to laissez-faire (unless inferior goods in social consumption were ruled out).[1]

This completes our proof and discussion of theorem 1. An intuitive explanation is perhaps in order. A *small* deviation as the result of the levy of a tax (subsidy) from an initial situation of *equality* of the values of two of the variables DRS, DRT and FRT does not entail welfare loss. So if the tax (subsidy) brings the value of the third variable closer to those of the two variables which were initially equal, the welfare gain on this account will constitute a net improvement in welfare. More than one form of tax (subsidy) may secure this result; and the levy of any one of these will be superior to laissez-faire.

But it should be noted that when only the policy that secures first-best can make DRS, DRT and FRT equal and adoption of this policy is ruled out, as when national monopoly power exists but a tariff cannot be levied, alternative policies cannot be ranked except with reference to the facts of a given situation. The corollary of this proposition is that when a second-best policy alone can secure

---

[1] Note that in the present case, dealing with a domestic consumption distortion, a production or factor-use tax-cum-subsidy policy may improve welfare, whereas case 1, dealing with a domestic production, did not admit to a consumption tax-cum-subsidy raising welfare above the laissez-faire level. The reason for this asymmetry is as follows. In the latter case, a consumption tax-cum-subsidy, whether small or large, cannot shift and hence cannot improve welfare. In the former case, however, a production or factor-use tax-cum-subsidy can affect consumption through its income effect. The level of such a tax-cum-subsidy at an infinitesimal rate cannot, of course, change welfare because the income effect is zero to a first order of approximation; but when the rate is large, welfare may improve if the function relating welfare and the rate of tax (subsidy) is not concave (a possibility introduced by the presence of goods inferior in social consumption).

equality of *DRS*, *DRT* and *FRT*, as when a distortionary wage differential cannot be directly attacked, the third-best policy cannot be determined *a priori*.

Theorem 2

Assume now that national monopoly power exists, and that there is a production externality or that factor taxes (subsidies) cannot be used to eliminate a distortionary wage differential. Then $DRT \neq DRS \neq FRT$. We rule out the case in which, by chance, $DRT = FRT$. So $p_f \neq p_t$, $dp_f \neq 0$ and $p_c = p_f$; and equation (1) reduces to

$$dU = U_2[dX_1(p_f - p_t) + (X_1 - C_1)dp_f]. \quad \ldots \ldots (5)$$

The simultaneous levy of both a tariff and a production tax (subsidy) would secure first-best in the case of a production externality and second-best in the case of a distortionary wage differential. But if only a tariff or a production tax (subsidy) is applied, there may be exactly offsetting changes in $dX_1(p_f - p_t)$ and $(X_1 - C_1)dp_f$, and welfare may not increase. So if both the policy measures needed to secure equality of *DRS*, *DRT* and *FRT* cannot be applied, no feasible intervention may exist that will raise welfare above the laissez-faire level.

REFERENCES

1. Bhagwati, Jagdish, and Ramaswami, V.K., 'Domestic Distortions, Tariffs and the Theory of Optimum Subsidy', *Journal of Political Economy*, Vol. LXXI, No. 1, February 1963, pp. 44–50.
2. Kemp, M. C. and Negishi, T., 'Domestic Distortions, Tariffs and the Theory of Optimum Subsidy', *Journal of Political Economy*, Vol. LXXVII, No. 6, November/December 1969, pp. 1011–13.

3. Welfare Maximization When Domestic Factor Movement Entails External Diseconomies[1]

Jagdish Bhagwati and the present author [1] and H. G. Johnson [5] have applied Paretian and 'second-best' welfare theory to show that the optimal means of handling a domestic distortion or externality is some form of intervention in the domestic eeonomy, and not restriction of foreign trade. This general principle is applicable to the problem of welfare maximization when the transfer of factors from the production of non-traded goods to that of exportables entails external diseconomies, for example because labour movement can be induced only by unemployment which results in loss of potential output. We prove that the optimal policy is to levy a consumption tax on exportables, and to restrict imports only to the extent justified on familiar optimum tariff grounds. Thereafter we comment on the pioneering analysis of this problem by M. F. W. Hemming and W. M. Corden [3].

Consider an economy in which labour alone is used to produce an exportable x (which also enters into domestic consumption) and a non-traded good h, under conditions of constant returns to scale. The wage rate and hence the supply prices of x and h are rigid, and we normalize these at unity by choice of units of quantity. The outputs of x and h are X and H. Given the initial distribution of the labour force between the two industries, full employment outputs of x and h are $\bar{X}$ and $\bar{H}$. Without loss of generality, we assume that each worker produces one unit of output *per* time-period, whether employed in the x or the h industry. If n workers are employed in the h industry, qn $(0<q<1)$ workers will shift to the x industry; and so the highest feasible output of x can be raised from $\bar{X}$ to $\bar{X} + qn$, if output of h is restricted to $\bar{H} - n$. We assume that the initial labour

---

[1] The author is indebted to J. Bhagwati, W. M. Corden, H. G. Johnson and T. N. Srinivasan for useful comments and verification of the analysis. The views expressed are personal.

allocation to the h industry is so large that it is never optimal to move labour to that industry.

An importable m also enters into consumption, the quantum of imports being M. The price in foreign currency of m is always unity, because foreign supply is perfectly elastic, and by choice of units of quantity.

The price in domestic currency of one unit of foreign currency, p, is a policy variable. In the absence of tariffs and subsidies the price in domestic currency of m is p, while the price in foreign currency of x is $1/p$

X_{fmax}, the foreign demand for x, varies directly with p; and we have

$$X_{fmax} = f(p), f'(p) > 0. \ldots \ldots \ldots \ldots (1)$$

If the difference between the maximum output of and home demand for x is less than X_{fmax} for given p, foreigners will get delayed deliveries, with home demand always being fully and promptly met.

The utility function is

$$U = U(X_d, M, H). \ldots \ldots \ldots \ldots (2)$$

This utility function is increasing in all arguments, concave, and differentiable as required. Some quantity of each good is assumed to be demanded, given any set of finite price ratios.[1] The marginal utility of any one of the goods increases as the consumption of either of the other two goods increases.[2]

We write

t_m for the rate of tax on imports of m,

t_x for the rate of tax on domestic consumption of x, and

U_x, U_m, and U_h for marginal utilities derived from the consumption of x, m and h.

The marginal conditions for consumer utility maximization are

$$\frac{U_m}{U_x} = \frac{P(1 + t_m)}{1 + t_x}, \frac{U_m}{U_h} = p(1 + t_m), \text{ and } \frac{U_x}{U_h} = 1 + t_x \ . \ . \ (3)$$

If B^* is the desired value of B, the trade balance in terms of domestic currency, we must have

$$B^* = X_f - pM \ldots \ldots \ldots \ldots \ldots (4)$$

[1] This assumption is made in order to rule out several boundary solutions and thereby simplify the analysis. It is not essential to our conclusions.

[2] This assumption rules out 'inferiority' of any of the goods.

31

c

Assuming that consumers spend factor incomes *plus* income subsidies received from the government, (4) will be met if the budget surplus (deficit) equals the desired trade surplus (deficit). The trade balance equals domestic output at factor cost *plus* government revenue (R) *minus* factor incomes minus government expenditure (E); and so

$$B = X_f + X_d + H + R - X_f - X_d - H - E = R - E = B^* \quad (5)$$

Thus if an initial situation is one of disequilibrium, the extent of change required in the excess of government revenue over government expenditure is determined solely by the trade balance desired to be secured. For the sake of simplicity, we assume that balanced trade is desired; our analysis can, however, readily be extended, without change in the conclusions, to the case in which a trade surplus or deficit is specified.

A FIXED EXCHANGE RATE

We first consider the case in which it is not politically feasible to change the exchange rate. In Figure 1 the quantities of x produced,

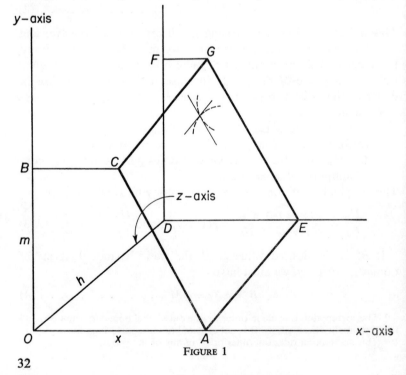

FIGURE 1

m imported and h produced are measured along the x-, y- and z-axes. If no h is produced, output of x can be OA. The economy can export x, in order to secure supplies of m, up to the ceiling $X_{fmax}(OB)$ for given p. This trading possibility is represented by AC, the slope of this line in the xy plane being $1/p$.

When $H = \bar{H}$, the output of h is OD. The highest feasible output of x shrinks to DE. The slope of AE in the xz plane is $1/q$, the rate of transformation in production between x and h. Trade is now possible along EG, whose slope in the xy plane is the same as that of AC; and maximum imports $DF = OB$.

The economy's consumption frontier subject to the domestic externality is the parallelogram $AEGC$. The optimal consumption point is that at which a community indifference surface (c.i.s.) is tangential to $AEGC$.

If a c.i.s. is tangential to the $AEGC$ plane at an interior point, then each line on the plane passing through the point is tangential to the c.i.s. So parallel lines to AE and EG on the $AEGC$ plane are tangents to the c.i.s., whose slopes at the tangency point in the xy and xz planes are therefore $1/p$ and $1/q$ respectively.

Therefore an optimal interior solution will be characterized by

$$\frac{U_m}{U_x} = p, \frac{U_x}{U_h} = \frac{1}{q}, \text{ and so } \frac{U_m}{U_h} = \frac{p}{q} \quad \ldots \ldots \ldots \text{(6)}$$

For this optimal interior equilibrium to be reached, imports of m and consumption of x must be taxed at the uniform rate $1/q - 1$. There will be some unemployment in the h industry.

If in the optimal solution $M < M_{max}$, but $H = \bar{H}$, the optimal consumption point is a point on EG other than G. Once more $U_m/U_x = p$; and $1 \leqslant U_x/U_h \leqslant 1/q$. Then optimal t_x and t_m will be such that $O \leqslant t_x = t_m \leqslant 1/q - 1$. Because we have assumed that it is never worthwhile to shift labour from the x to the h industry, U_x/U_h will not be less than 1. As $H = \bar{H}$ there is no unemployment in this solution.

Now suppose that in the optimal solution $M = M_{max}$. If optimal $H < \bar{H}$, the optimal consumption point lies on CG but is not G. Then optimal $t_x = 1/q - 1$, and optimal $t_m \geqslant 1/q - 1$ and must secure $M = M_{max}$. If $H = \bar{H}$, so that the optimal consumption point is G, consumption of x must be left free or taxed at a rate not greater than $1/q - 1$ so as to secure $H = \bar{H}$, and t_m must be set at the level at which $M = M_{max}$.

The optimal consumption point cannot lie on the boundaries AE and AC, as we have assumed that some quantity of each good is always consumed.

Thus optimality requires that rates of substitution in consumption should equal rates of transformation through production or trade, except in boundary solutions where appropriate inequalities must be satisfied.

A VARIABLE EXCHANGE RATE

We now allow for adjustment of the exchange rate as a policy measure. In Figure 2 we once more measure production of x, con-

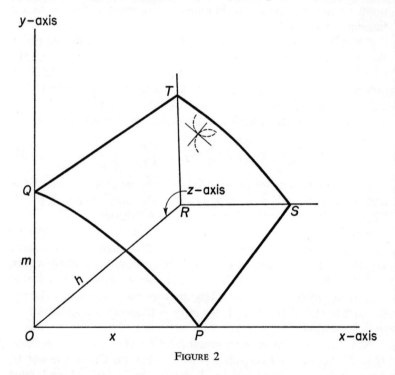

FIGURE 2

sumption of m and production of h along the x-, y-, and z- axes. If no h is produced, output of x is OP, and the economy can trade along PQ. We assume that X_{fmax}/p rises monotonically at a decreasing rate as p is increased, and PQ is therefore continuous and

34

strictly convex.[1] $OR = \bar{H}$, and the economy can trade along ST when $H = \bar{H}$. The slope of SP in the xz plane is $1/q$. The economy's consumption frontier is $PSTQ$. Given our assumption that some quantity of each good is always demanded, the optimal solution cannot lie on the boundaries QT, PQ and PS; it must therefore be an interior one or lie on ST (but not at S or T). It is easily verified that, in an interior solution $U_x/U_h = 1/q$.

The rate of transformation of x into m through production and trade is, however, no longer equal to p. When the exchange rate is a policy variable, it is sub-optimal to allow excess foreign demand for exports to prevail; if there is such excess foreign demand, currency appreciation will result in larger imports with no change in exports. So we must always have $X_f = X_{fmax}$. An increase in X_f in order to raise M, while keeping trade balanced, entails a devaluation and a consequent deterioration in the terms of trade. Differentiating X_f/p with respect to X_f, we find that we must have

$$\frac{U_m}{U_x} = \frac{p^2}{p - X_f\, \partial p/\partial X_f} \quad \cdots \cdots \cdots \quad (7)$$

Thus in the optimal interior solution $t_x = 1/q$ and

$$t_m = \frac{p - pq + qX_f\, \partial p/\partial X_f}{q(p - X_f\, \partial p/\partial X_f)} \quad \cdots \cdots \quad (8)$$

The expression (8) for t_m is simply the familiar optimum tariff. In an interior solution, there must be some unemployment because $H < \bar{H}$.

Full employment can prevail if the optimal solution lies along ST. Optimal t_x may be zero or positive but less than $1/q - 1$. Optimal t_m will be such that (7) holds.

Thus imports must always be taxed at the rate that is optimal for the exercise of national monopoly power; and once more there must be equality (or appropriate inequality in a boundary solution) between the consumer price ratio of the exportable and the non-

---

[1] If this assumption does not hold, PQ, ST and corresponding curves for values of h other than O and $\bar{H}$ will have concave and/or straight line bits. The concave stretch of such a curve cannot lie on the consumption frontier, for the economy can consume more of both m and x, and the same amount of h, by appreciating the currency and reducing exports. The consumption frontier will in this case be discontinuous.

35

traded good on the one hand, and the transformation ratio between these goods in production on the other.

CONCLUDING OBSERVATIONS

Hemming and Corden assumed, in their pioneering analysis of this problem, that the only policy instruments available were import restrictions—which in the present context are fully equivalent to import duties—and deflation or reflation. Given this choice of policy variables, their conclusion that it is likely to be desirable to restrict imports more than is warranted on optimum tariff grounds is entirely correct.[1] But the assumption that consumption taxes cannot be levied is unrealistic for developed economies such as the United Kingdom, in which tax authorities have long experience of the levy of purchase or other consumption taxes. We have shown that when levy of consumption taxes is feasible, trade restriction beyond the point justified for the exercise of national monopoly power is sub-optimal. The Hemming–Corden policy recommendations may, however, be valid for some underdeveloped countries in which taxation of consumption may not be feasible.

Hemming and Corden spoke of deflation or reflation as the means of securing optimal unemployment. We have shown that the optimal budget surplus or deficit is determined solely by the trade balance desired, and it has therefore nothing to do with the level of unemployment. It is the variation by means of taxation of the product price ratios confronting consumers that secures optimal unemployment.[2]

[1] It follows directly from second-best theory that if the marginal rate of substitution in consumption and the marginal rate of transformation in production between the exportable and the non-traded goods necessarily differ, then the optimal marginal rate of substitution in consumption between the exportable and the importable will not be the marginal rate of transformation between these goods through trade. When only trade taxes can be levied, a community indifference surface will not be tangential to, but will intersect, the consumption frontier at the optimal consumption point. Hemming and Corden are in error in treating the exportable and the non-traded good as a single commodity in their geometric analysis, and in speaking of tangency of an indifference curve with the consumption frontier (balance-of-payments improvement locus, in their terminology) in the optimal solution.

[2] If a budget balance equal to the desired trade balance is maintained, and optimal taxes are levied, divergence of actual from optimal unemployment will be inconsistent with equilibrium in all markets. If the market for h is in balance with employment and output of h above (below) optimal levels, consumption of x and m must also be above (below) optimal levels for (3) to be met, as no good is 'inferior'. Consumption of all goods above optimal levels is not feasible. If output of h is less than optimal, output of x must be more than

We have followed Hemming and Corden in assuming that unemployment is a prerequisite for labour movement. If it is assumed instead that labour movement entails retraining for a fraction $1 - q$ of the time-period, that workers do not produce during the training period, and that training costs are not reflected in market prices, our results continue to hold, with retraining taking the place of unemployment.

A fuller analysis would take account of labour movement in response to unemployment and/or the gains from retraining not only in the current time-period but in future time-periods also. Thus the assumption that we have made, following Hemming and Corden, that *permanent* unemployment is necessary to secure a *once-for-all* movement of labour is clearly unrealistic, and should be modified to allow for shift of all or most of the initially unemployed labour over a certain number of time-periods. This is likely to weaken the case for intervention to shift demand towards non-traded goods.

REFERENCES

1. Bhagwati, J. and Ramaswami, V. K., 'Domestic Distortions, Tariffs, and the Theory of Optimum Subsidy', *Journal of Political Economy*, Vol. LXXI, No. 1, February 1963, pp. 44–50.
2. Corden, W. M., 'The Geometric Representation of Policies to attain Internal and External Balance', *Review of Economic Studies*, Vol. XXVIII, No. 75, 1960–1, pp. 1–22.
3. Hemming, M. F. W. and Corden, W. M., 'Import Restriction as an Instrument of Balance-of-Payments Policy', *Economic Journal*, Vol. LXVIII, No. 271, September 1958, pp. 483–510.
4. Johnson, H. G., 'Towards a General Theory of the Balance of Payments', in his *International Trade and Economic Growth: Studies in Pure Theory*, Cambridge, 1961.
5. Johnson, H. G., 'Optimal Trade Intervention in the Presence of Domestic Distortions', in R. E. Caves, P. B. Kenen and H. G. Johnson (ed.), *Trade, Growth, and the Balance of Payments, Essays in Honor of Gottfried Haberler*, Chicago, 1965.
6. Meade, J. E., *The Balance of Payments*, London, 1951.
7. Meade, J. E., *Trade and Welfare*, London, 1955.

---

optimal; and there will be excess supply of at least one tradeable if consumption of x and m is below optimal levels. An adjustment process whereby the market mechanism ensures that, even if wrong decisions are initially taken, the optimal solution is eventually reached, can easily be described.

4. Optimal Subsidies and Taxes When Some Factors are Traded

I

Trade taxes are widely used to collect revenue. The levy, instead of a uniform consumption tax, would secure revenue without welfare loss, if factor supplies are inelastic. It is, however, often not feasible, particularly in underdeveloped countries, to tax the consumption of much of home output. It is therefore of practical importance to determine the optimal policies for collecting specified revenue through trade taxes. Yet, while the optimum tariff for the exercise of national monopoly power has been extensively and elegantly analysed in the literature, there has been little discussion of the optimum revenue tariff.[1] Our first task in this paper is to analyse this problem, taking trade in intermediate goods into account. As has been pointed out by Bhagwati[1] in his invaluable survey [1] p. 3), the assumption that only final goods are traded has been a central limitation of trade theory in a real world in which a large portion of world trade consists of intermediate goods.

Consider a small country confronted by given world prices[2] and endowed with a single factor, labour (L), which is inelastic in supply, immobile between countries, and always fully employed.[3] This country produces a good x solely for export, makes all it needs of a consumer good c_d, and relies wholly on imports for supplies of another consumer good c_i. Quantities of x, c_d and c_i are denoted by X, C_d and C_i. The production of x or c_d requires both labour and a

---

[1] Johnson (1951–2) [4] sets out the formula for the maximum revenue tariff when national monopoly power exists. The problem discussed by Mead ([10] pp. 186–99) and Kindleberger ([9] pp. 223–4) is the optimal mix of consumption, production, and trade taxes when these taxes can be levied on some but not on all commodities. Kemp ([8] p. 183) sets before the reader the problem of determining the optimal set of tariffs to raise given revenue, but provides no solution.

[2] There is thus no scope for the exercise of national monopoly power. We choose units of quantity for all tradeables such that world prices are unity.

[3] The total supply of labour by choice of units is unity.

wholly imported factor, metal, the quantum of metal imports being M. Trade is assumed to be balanced,[1] so $X = C_i + M$. The production functions for x and c_d exhibit constant returns to scale and are twice continuously differentiable and concave. They are $f(m_x)$ and $g(m_d)$, where m_x and m_d are metal/labour ratios in the production of x and c_d.[2] The utility function $U(C_d, C_i)$ is increasing in both arguments, twice continuously differentiable and concave.[3]

Under free trade, technique in export production will be such that the marginal value product of metal at world prices is unity. This determines the wage rate (w); using asterisks as superscripts to denote the free trade values of variables, we write w^* for the free trade wage rate. Technique in making c_d is uniquely determined, given the factor/price ratio $w^*/1$, and so is p, the price of a unit of c_d. The labour L_d devoted to making c_d, will be such that the ratio of the marginal utilities of the two goods equals the product/price ratio; $U_i/U_d = 1/p$ in equilibrium, where U_i and U_d are marginal utilities derived from the consumption of c_i and c_d, respectively.

The government now has to collect revenue (R) equal to a specified fraction (π) of the wage bill through trade taxes alone for redistribution to consumers.[4] Revenue collection entails production cost due to departure from free-trade techniques in production and/or consumption cost because the product/price ratio confronting consumers is not at the free-trade level.[5] Our problem is to determine the optimal tax policy which secures specified revenue with the least welfare loss, taking both production and consumption costs of the tariff into account. We first prove that is it optimal to maintain the free-trade technique in export production; if, initially, metal used to make exports is taxed while exports are free of tax or subsidy, welfare can be raised by abolishing the tax on metal used to make exports and adjusting taxes on imports for home use to make up the revenue loss. We next show that the widely accepted rule of

---

[1] This assumption is relaxed in Appendix A.

[2] It is also assumed that the marginal physical product of a factor in the production of either good tends to zero (infinity) as its relative quantity tends to infinity (zero).

[3] It is further assumed that the marginal utility of either good tends to infinity (zero) as the consumption of that good tends to zero (infinity), and the marginal utility of either good increases as the consumption of the other good increases.

[4] We assume that revenue is redistributed to consumers, for the sake of analytical simplicity.

[5] Johnson ([5], [6]) elucidates the production and consumption costs of a tariff.

thumb that taxes on imports for home use should be uniform is erroneous.

We write t_x and t_d for the rates of tax on imports of metal to make x and c_d, respectively; t_i for the rate of tax on imports of c_i; and t for the rate of subsidy on exports of x. Negative t_x, t_d, and t_i denote subsidy rates, and negative t denotes a tax rate.

The marginal conditions for profit maximization are:

$$(1 + t)f'(m_x) = 1 + t_x, \quad \ldots \ldots \ldots \quad (1)$$

$$(1 + t)[f(m_x) - m_x f'(m_x)] = w, \quad \ldots \ldots \quad (2)$$

$$pg'(m_d) = 1 + t_d, \quad \ldots \ldots \ldots \ldots \quad (3)$$

and

$$p[g(m_d) - m_d g'(m_d)] = w \quad \ldots \ldots \ldots \quad (4)$$

As $C_d = L_d g(m_d)$ and $C_i = X - M = (1 - L_d)[f(m_x) - m_x] - L_d m_d$, the utility function can be written in the form

$$U\{L_d g(m_d), (1 - L_d)[f(m_x) - m_x] - L_d m_d\}. \quad \ldots \ldots \quad (5)$$

The marginal condition for utility maximization is

$$\frac{U_i}{U_d} = \frac{1 + t_i}{p} \quad \ldots \ldots \ldots \ldots \ldots \quad (6)$$

given the assumptions regarding U, $C_i > 0$ and $0 < L_d < 1$. For a feasible solution, we must also have

$$1 + t, \ 1 + t_x, \ 1 + t_d, \ 1 + t_i, p, w, m_d, m_x \geqq 0 \ \ldots \ (7)$$

The revenue constraint is

$$-t(1 - L_d)f(m_x) + t_x(1 - L_d)m_x + t_d L_d m_d$$
$$+ t_i\{(1 - L_d)[f(m_x) - m_x] - L_d m_d\} = \pi w = R \ \ldots \ (8)$$

We have six equations, (1) through (4) and (6) and (8), and nine unknowns. We use the equations to solve uniquely for t, t_x, t_d, t_i, p, and w in terms of m_d, m_x, and L_d. Then, feasible values of m_d, m_x, and L_d are those for which (7) holds.

Given $m_d \geqq 0$, $m_x \geqq 0$, $1 > L_d > 0$, and $(1 - L_d)[f(m_x) - m_x]$

$-L_d m_d > 0$, equations (1) through (4) and (6) determine $(1 + t_d)/p$, w/p, $(1 + t_x)/(1 + t)$, and $(1 + t_i)/p$ uniquely. Hence, if choice of m_d, m_x, and L_d results in non-negative w with (8) being met, then (7) is also met. Now (8) can be rewritten[1] as (8') below.

$$w\left\{\frac{\dfrac{U_i}{U_d} \cdot C_i + C_d - (1 + \pi)[g(m_d) - m_d g'(m_d)]}{g(m_d) - m_d g'(m_d)}\right\} = 0 \qquad (8')$$

The term $g(m_d) - m_d g'(m_d)$—the marginal physical product of labour in industry c_d—is always finite and positive. If (8') is to be met with positive w, the expression in braces in the numerator, for which we shall write N, must be equal to zero.[2]

We wish to maximize the utility function (5) subject to $N = 0$, $1 > L_d > 0$, $m_d \geqq 0$, $m_x \geqq 0$, $C_i > 0$. Suppose that for some non-negative L_d, m_d, and m_x these constraints are met (m_x being different from m_x^*). Given these values of L_d and m_d and therefore of C_d, we can maximize C_i, and hence welfare, by changing m_x to m_x^*, given that $C_i = (1 - L_d)[f(m_x) - m_x] - L_d m_d$. If N continues to be non-negative,[3] the optimal value of m_x is clearly m_x^*.

---

[1] The equation was derived thus:

$$(1 + t_d)L_d m_a = \frac{w L_d g(m_d)}{g(m_d) - m_d g'(m_d)} - w L_d$$

from (3) and (4),

$$[(1 + t_x)m_x - (1 + t)f(m_x)](1 - L_d) = - w(1 - L_d)$$

from (1) and (2), and

$$1 + t_i = \frac{U_i}{U_d} \cdot \frac{w}{g(m_d) - m_d g'(m_d)}$$

from (4) and (6).

Substitute in (8) after adding and subtracting $(1 - L_d)[f(m_x) - m_x] - L_d m_d$ to its left-hand side, and thereafter substitute C_d for $L_d g(m_d)$ and C_i for $(1 - L_d)[f(m_x) - m_x] - L_d m_d$.

[2] The solution $w = 0$ must be ruled out, for it can be verified from (1) through (4) that if $w = 0$ all factor and product prices are zero, and no determinate equilibrium exists.

[3] If $N > 0$, more than specified revenue will be collected, and the excess can be returned to taxpayers.

But suppose that N becomes negative. This must be because the fall in U_i/U_d when C_i is raised with C_d held constant outweighs the rise in C_i; $g(m_d) - m_d g'(m_d)$ does not change for we have not altered m_d. In that case, we can hold m_d and C_i constant when we change m_x to m_x^*. Less labour is now needed in industry x to secure the net exports to pay for unchanged C_i and the metal hitherto used to make c_d; we can raise L_d and therefore C_d. Then U_i/U_d is higher, as C_i is unchanged while C_d is larger, and N is greater. We have therefore raised welfare while meeting the revenue constraint. This completes our proof that it is optimal to maintain the free trade technique in export production.

Let us now set $t = t_x = 0$ so that $w = w^*$, and consider the optimal values of t_d and t_i.[1] For this purpose we use Figure 1, in which OT (OT_1) is the quantity of c_i (c_d) that can be consumed if there is no consumption of the other consumer good and if the free trade technique is used to make c_d. The slope of TT_1 is the free trade product/price ratio, and under free trade the consumption point is P. One way of collecting revenue is to set $t_d = 0$, thus maintaining the free trade technique in producing c_d, and to set t_i at the level that secures the specified revenue. Consumption will then be at Q, the point on TT_1 at which an indifference curve is tangent to a price line with the slope $p^*/1 + t_i$. This policy entails consumption cost but no production cost, and the welfare loss resulting from its adoption sets a ceiling to the welfare cost of revenue collection. It may, however, be possible to raise welfare by levying a tax at a low rate on imports of metal to make c_d, thus accepting some production cost, and lowering t_i to the extent consistent with collection of the specified revenue. The quantity of c_d that can be produced and consumed if there is no consumption of c_i is now OT_2, and consumption will be at the point R on TT_2 at which an indifference curve is tangent to a price line which is steeper than the price line with consumption at Q. Because of the change in the slope of the price line, R may lie on a higher indifference curve than Q, as in

[1] Choice of w is arbitrary because (8) is homogeneous of degree 1 in the variables $1 + t$, $1 + t_x$, $1 + t_d$, $1 + t_i$, p, and w. If the proportionate change in $1 + t$, $1 + t_x$, $1 + t_d$, and $1 + t_i$ is λ, it is clear from (1) through (4) and (6) that the quantities of each good produced and consumed do not change and that the proportionate change in p and w is λ. The quantities t, t_x, t_d, and t_i change to $\lambda(1 + t) - 1$, $\lambda(1 + t_x) - 1$, $\lambda(1 + t_d) - 1$, and $\lambda(1 + t_i) - 1$. As the levy of a tax *cum* subsidy at the rate $\lambda - 1$ does not change revenue, the proportionate change in revenue is also λ.

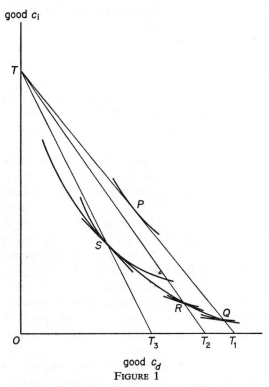

good c_i

good c_d

FIGURE 1

Figure 1, though TT_2 is inside OTT_1. By continuing to lower t_i and to raise t_d while meeting the revenue constraint, we can trace the curve QRS—the locus of points such as Q and R—which is the consumption frontier subject to the revenue constraint. The optimal consumption point is S, at which an indifference curve is tangent to QRS; beyond this point, the gain in welfare due to lower t_i reducing consumption cost is less than the welfare loss resulting from the higher production cost entailed by larger t_d.

There is no particular reason why the optimal values of t_i and t^p should be the same. It is often asserted that a uniform tax on all imports for home use is optimal, because this equates the marginal utilities derived from alternative uses of foreign exchange. For this proposition to be valid, foreign exchange availability must be invariant with respect to tax changes. In general, however, the allocation of domestic factors to export production and hence foreign exchange availability vary when tax rates are changed, and

43

this is why duties on imports for home use are unlikely to be uniform in the second-best revenue tariff.[1,2]

II

We now turn to problems of output diversification. Underdeveloped countries often wish to diversify output because of the uncertainties considered to be associated with production of a limited number of commodities, mainly for export. They desire to make new items, whether for export or for the home market. Someimes, however, the objective is the autarkic one of producing new items for home consumption only. We discuss the optimal means of achieving these alternative objectives, assuming that any revenue needed can be raised in a non-distortionary way and that the policy instruments available are output subsidies and trade and consumption taxes. We use the model of Section I with a modification. We now assume that x alone is made under free trade, c_d and c_i being imported, and we allow for the possibility of producing c_i at home, the production function for this good having the same characteristics as those for x and c_d.[3] Objective 1 is output worth θ at world prices of c_d and/or c_i *for home use or for export*, while the alternative objective 2 is production worth θ at world prices of c_d and/or c_i *for home use alone*. We prove the following. (1) Given objective 1, the optimal policy is to hold factor prices at the free trade level and to subsidize output of that good other than x (which we assume to be c_d) in whose production the unit cost is least, so as to maintain the free trade product/price ratio in consumption.[4] (2) If at least θ of c_d is consumed at home under policy (1), an equivalent result is secured by levy of an import duty on c_d and c_i at the uniform rate just sufficient to induce production of c_d. Either this policy or policy (1) is also

---

[1] A counter-example to prove that optimal duties on imports for home use need not be equal is provided in Appendix B.

[2] Kindleberger ([9] pp. 223–4) defines a tariff for revenue only as being one that has consumption cost but does not affect production. He concludes that a uniform tax on imports is not optimal, because it is likely to distort production. The definition is unacceptable, because while production changes are not an objective of the revenue tariff, there is no reason why they should not be accepted if, as a result, the welfare loss due to revenue collection is minimized.

[3] The unit of quantity for c_d has a world price of unity.

[4] That an output subsidy is the optimal means of diversifying production when the terms of trade are fixed was shown by Corden [3]. See also Johnson [7].

optimal to secure objective 2. (3) If, however, c_d is exported under policy (1), that policy is superior to alternative policies, given objective 1. The optimal policy to achieve objective 2 is to hold factor prices at the free trade level, to levy import duties on c_d and c_i at rates just sufficient to induce production, and to levy an optimal consumption tax on c_i; use of import duties alone yields lower welfare.

Suppose that the output of c_d is θ and that c_i is not made. With any given L_d, m_d foreign exchange available to import c_i and additional supplies of c_d is $(1 - L_d) [f(m_x) - m_x] - L_d m_d$. Differentiating partially with respect to m_x, we have $m_x = m_x^*$ for a maximum value and we set $w = w^*$. Differentiating partially with respect to m_d, $\partial L_d / \partial m_d = L_d / [f(m_x^*) - m_x^* + m_d]$ for a maximum value. As $L_d g(m_d) = \theta$,

$$g'(m_d) = - \frac{g(m_d)}{L_d} \cdot \frac{\partial L_d}{\partial m_d} = \frac{g(m_d)}{f(m_x^*) - m_x^* + m_d} = \frac{w^* + p m_d g'(m_d)}{p[f(m_x^*) - m_x^* + m_d]}$$

from (4). Hence, $pg'(m_d) [f(m_x^*) - m_x^*] = w^*$; and as $f(m_x^*) - m_x^* = w^*$, $pg'(m_d) = 1$. The optimal factor prices in the manufacture of c_d are thus w^* and 1. Similarly, if c_i is made, the optimal factor prices will once more be w^* and 1. By assumption, the unit cost u_d of c_d at these factor prices is less than the unit cost u_i of c_i. Production of a unit of c_i instead of a unit of c_d to meet an output constraint reduces foreign exchange available for imports by $u_i - u_d$. A subsidy to specified output of c_d at the rate $u_d - 1$ secures objective 1 at the least cost. If consumers demand at least θ of c_d at the world price ratio, levy of import duty on c_d and c_i at the rate $u_d - 1$ is an equivalent policy.

It may be, however, that c_d is exported when its output is subsidized. In that case, grant of an output subsidy is superior to alternative policies when objective 1 is specified, for levy of import duties and/or consumption taxes result in higher production cost due to c_i being produced and/or consumption cost because of departure from the free trade product/price ratio in consumption.

If the autarkic objective 2 is stipulated, we note that in the optimal solution $p_d / p_i = 1 - u_i + u_d$, where p_d and p_i are the domestic prices of the two goods. The resources released when one unit less of c_d is made are inadequate to produce an additional unit of c_i to meet the output constraint and need to be supplemented by a fall of $u_i - u_d$ in imports of c_i. Now, if import duties alone are levied, the duty on c_i must be $u_i - 1$ and the price u_i for market equilibrium when this good is both produced and imported. The price of c_d is its unit cost u_d when it is prohibitively protected. Good c_d is then relatively too expensive from the social point of view, for

$$(1 - u_i + u_d) - \frac{u_d}{u_i} = - \frac{(u_i - u_d)(u_i - 1)}{u_i} < 0,$$

as $u_i > u_d > 1$. It is easily verified that an additional levy of a tax on each unit of c_i consumed at the rate $[(u_i - u_d)(u_i - 1)]/(1 - u_i + u_d)$ secures equality of p_d/p_i and $1 - u_i + u_d$. If only import duties are levied, the product/price ratio will not equal the marginal cost ratio from the social point of view, and welfare will be lower.[1]

In Figure 2, OP is the quantity θ of c_d, OT is the quantity of c_d that can be consumed if there is no consumption of c_i, and the slope of TT_1T_2 is the free trade product/price ratio. If at this price ratio the consumption point is C_1, it is optimal to subsidize output of c_d or to tax import of c_d and c_i at the rate $u_d - 1$, given either objective. If, however, an indifference curve is tangent to TT_1T_2 to the left of T_1, say, at C_2, this consumption point can be reached only if objective 1 is specified and output of c_d is subsidized; this good will then be exported. The consumption frontier when objective 2 is stipulated is TT_1T_3, and levy of optimal import duties and consumption tax secures equilibrium at C_3, where an indifference curve is tangent to T_1T_3. Levy of import duties alone results in consumption at, say, C_4, where an indifference curve cuts the consumption frontier.

III

We now offer some concluding observations.

We have shown that inputs used in export production must be free of duty in the second-best revenue tariff. While it is common practice to grant drawbacks of duty paid on the import content of exports, there are often irrational requirements, such as imported input must be physically embodied in the export good. From the

[1] Cooper and Massell [2] assert that an efficient tariff is one that maximizes national income at world prices subject to specified output of protected goods. This proposition is valid only on their special assumption that the quantities demanded of each good are invariant with reference to relative prices, which eliminates the consumption cost of protection.

good c_i

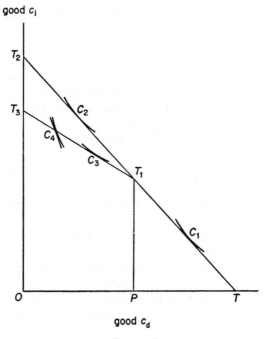

good c_d

FIGURE 2

economic point of view there is no difference between fuel consumed in making a product and components built into it.[1]

We have also proved that optimal revenue duties on imports for home use will in general not be uniform. This does not, of course, mean that complex tariffs in the real world, which have been framed largely in response to pressures of interested groups, are optimal. What our conclusion suggests is that revenue tariffs should be based on objective empirical research.

When countries claim that they need trade taxes to collect revenue, they should be under an obligation to show that alternative means of raising revenue are inferior. It is remarkable that while multiple

[1] There are, no doubt, practical difficulties in verifying the import content of exports. Production for export in free trade zones is a convenient solution. High tariff countries are likely to find that the setting up of such zones expands exports. In many cases, sample inspection of exports at the frontier will suffice to determine the production process and hence import content. While no system can be perfect, the objective should be to make imported inputs available to exporters at world prices to the fullest extent practicable.

D

exchange rate and import control systems are subject to international review, countries can levy any tariffs they like on items not bound in GATT negotiations. As a result, many countries, some of which are very rich, levy tariffs which probably both reduce national welfare unnecessarily and worsen international income distribution.

If a government deficit-finances expenditure and the central bank makes an equal profit by setting multiple exhange rates for different categories of trade transactions, this is equivalent to the levy of a revenue tariff and our conclusions apply fully. If, on the other hand, government expenditure is deficit financed and quantitative restrictions are applied to imports, identical results can be secured only if the level of expenditure is the same as when tariffs are levied. For this to happen, import licencees must save all their windfall profits. And as they probably will not do so, a secondary round of price increases which induces further savings through a change in income distribution or other effects is likely to take place. Needless to say, exporters should be allowed to import inputs freely if quantitative restrictions are irrationally preferred to tariffs or multiple exchange rates. In practice, import control systems often impede exports, because exporters have to use high-cost domestic substitutes for imported materials.

When a country wishes to diversify production, output subsidies—and not protection—are called for. When the objective is the irrational one of autarky, not only protective duties but also consumption taxes will be ingredients of the optimal policy. Imported inputs used by protected industries must be free of duty. Taxation of such inputs is sub-optimal, because domestic factors are then diverted from making exports to wasteful substitution of imported inputs.

APPENDIX A

In this appendix we relax the assumption that trade is balanced. Assume that the magnitude of a specified capital inflow (Δ) or outflow ($-\Delta$) is independent of the trade policy followed. Loans or gifts are received from or made to foreigners only by the private sector. We show that specified revenue can be collected without departure from free trade first-best if $\Delta < 0$ or if $\Delta > 0$ and the revenue requirement at free trade prices is less than the capital inflow.

Consider the levy of a uniform import tax (subsidy) and export subsidy (tax) at the rate $t(-t)$. Then $R = t(M + C_i - Y) = t\Delta$. The revenue required is πw; and as $w = w^*(1 + t)$, $\pi w^*(1 + t) = t\Delta$. But $1 + t$ has to be positive for feasibility. Hence, $t > 0$ if $\Delta > 0$, and $t < 0$ if $\Delta < 0$.

The solution for t is $t = \pi w^*/(\Delta - \pi w^*)$. Hence, the condition $t < 0$ will be met for all $\Delta < 0$. But if $\Delta > 0$, $t < 0$ only if $\pi w^* \geqq \Delta$.

The crucial assumption in the above proof, that the magnitude of capital flows is independent of the trade policy followed, is of course unlikely to hold in the real world. It may be noted, however, that levy of a uniform tax *cum* subsidy by, say, a capital-importing country does not alter the profit rate on investment in that country. Tax on the capital inflow is offset by subsidy on capital servicing charges. The amount that the foreign investor must provide in his currency to set up a given plant will, on the other hand, be higher. At any rate, levy of such a uniform tax *cum* subsidy can usefully be considered by countries receiving significant amounts from abroad by way of capital inflow or migrants' remittances.

If $\Delta > 0$ and $\pi w^* \geqq \Delta$, only a second-best solution is possible. Our analysis of the balanced trade case can easily be extended to show that the free trade technique must be maintained in export production in this second-best solution.

APPENDIX B

In this appendix we provide a counter example to show that duties on imports for home use need not be uniform in the second-best revenue tariff. We assume that trade is balanced. Consider the following utility and production functions:

$$U = (C_d^{-\rho} + C_i^{-\rho})^{-1/\rho} \quad \dots\dots\dots\dots\dots \quad \text{(B1)}$$

where $\rho \geqq -1$, and

$$G = L_d^{1-\alpha} M_d^{\alpha} \quad \dots\dots\dots\dots\dots\dots \quad \text{(B2)}$$

where $0 < \alpha < 1$. No specific production function need be assumed for x. It can easily be shown that if $\rho = 0$, that is, if the elasticity of substitution in the utility function is unity, then optimal $t_d = t_i$. We now prove that if the elasticity of substitution in the utility function is less than unity, then t_d is less than t_i in the optimal solution. Our method is to suppose that $t_d = t_i$ in an optimal solution and to prove that this is impossible, as welfare can be raised while meeting the revenue constraint by reducing t_d and raising t_i.

Partially differentiating (B1) with respect to C_d and C_i, we ascertain that $U_i/U_d = (C_d/C_i)^{\rho+1} = (1 + t_i)/p$ from (6). If $t_d = t_i$ in the optimal solution, $(1 + t_i)/p = (1 + t_d)/p = g'(m_d)$ from (3). Therefore,

$$\frac{U_i}{U_d} = \left(\frac{C_d}{C_i}\right)^{\rho+1} = \frac{1 + t_i}{p} = \frac{1 + t_d}{p} = g'(m_d). \quad \dots \quad \text{(B3)}$$

Now change t_d, L_d, C_i t_i, and M_d by δ, γ, μ, ϵ, and η, respectively. By the balance of payments constraint, $-(1 - L_d - \gamma)w^* + (M_a + \eta) + (C_i + \eta) = 0$, and $-(1 - L_d)w^* + M_a + C_i = 0$; hence, $\mu = -\eta - \gamma w^*$. Now

$$\frac{g(m_d) - m_a g'(m_d)}{g'(m_d)} = \frac{w^*}{1 + t_d}$$

But

$$\frac{g(m_d) - m_d g'(m_d)}{g'(m_d)} = \frac{(1 - a)m_d}{a},$$

or

$$m_d = \frac{a}{1 - a} \cdot \frac{w^*}{1 + t_d}$$

This implies $\Delta m_d = - m_d \delta/(1 + t_d)$. By definition, $L_d a m_d = M_d$. Hence, $\Delta M_d = \eta = m_d \Delta L_d + L_d \Delta m_d$, or $\eta = \gamma m_d - \delta M_d/(1 + y_d)$. This implies that

$$\mu = - \gamma(m_d + w^*) + \frac{\delta L_d m_d}{1 + t_d} \quad \dots\dots\dots\dots \text{(B4)}$$

For the revenue constraint to be met,

$$(M_d + \eta)(t_d + \delta) + (C_i + \mu)(t_d + \epsilon) = M_d t_d + C_i t_d$$

Ignoring second-order terms,

$$\delta M_d + t_d\left(\gamma m_d - \frac{\delta L_d m_d}{1 + t_d}\right) + C_i \epsilon + t_d\left[- \gamma(m_d + w^*) + \frac{\delta L_d m_d}{1 + t_d}\right] = 0,$$

or $\epsilon = (\gamma t_d w^* - \delta M_d)/C_i$.

Now from (B3), $(\rho + 1)(\log C_d - \log C_i) = \log (1 + t_i) - \log p$. Hence

$$(\rho + 1)\left(\frac{\Delta C_d}{C_d} - \frac{\Delta C_i}{C_i}\right) = - \frac{\Delta p}{p} + \frac{\Delta t_i}{1 + t_i} \quad \dots\dots\dots \text{(B5)}$$

Now $C_d = L_d g(m_d) = L_d m_d^a$, and

$$\Delta C_d = m_d^a \Delta L_d + \alpha L_d m_d^{a-1} \Delta m_d$$

$$= \gamma m_d^a + \alpha L_d m_d^{a-1}\left(- \frac{m_d \delta}{1 + t_d}\right) = m_d\left(\gamma - \frac{a\delta L_d}{1 + t_d}\right)$$

Therefore,

$$\frac{\Delta C_d}{C_d} = \frac{\gamma}{L_d} - \frac{a\delta}{1 + t_d} \quad \dots\dots\dots\dots \text{(B6)}$$

From (B4) and (B6),

$$\frac{\Delta C_d}{C_d} - \frac{\Delta C_i}{C_i} = \gamma\left(\frac{1}{L_d} + \frac{m_d + w^*}{C_i}\right) - \frac{\delta}{1 + t_d}\left(a + \frac{L_d m_d}{C_i}\right) \quad \dots \text{(B7)}$$

Now

$$p = \frac{w^*}{g(m_d) - m_d g'(m_d)} = \frac{w^*}{1 - a} \cdot m_d^{-a},$$

and

$$\frac{\Delta p}{p} = -\frac{a \Delta m_d}{m_d)} = \frac{a\delta}{1 + t_d}.$$

$$\frac{\Delta t_i}{1 + t_i} = \frac{\epsilon}{1 + t_d} = \frac{\gamma t_d w^* - \delta L_d m_d}{C_i(1 + t_d)}.$$

Therefore,

$$, \qquad -\frac{\Delta p}{p} + \frac{\Delta t_i}{1 + t_i} = \frac{1}{1 + t_d}\left[\frac{\gamma t_d w^*}{C_i} - \delta\left(a + \frac{L_d m_d}{C_i}\right)\right] \quad \ldots (B8)$$

Substituting from (B7) and (B8) into (B5) and rearranging terms,

$$\gamma\left[\frac{\rho + 1}{L_d} + \frac{(\rho + 1)(m_d + w^*)}{C_i} - \frac{t_d}{1 + t_d} \cdot \frac{w^*}{C_i}\right] = \frac{\rho\delta}{1 + t_d}\left(a + \frac{L_d m_d}{C_i}\right)$$

Now

$$(\rho + 1)\left(\frac{1}{L_d} + \frac{m_d + w^*}{C_i}\right) = \frac{\rho + 1}{L_d C_i}(C_i + L_d m_d + w^* L_d);$$

and as trade is balanced, $C_i + L_d m_d + w^* L_d = C_i + M_d + w^* L_d = w^*$. Hence,

$$\gamma\left[\frac{w^*(\rho + 1)}{L_d C_i} - \frac{w^* t_d}{C_i(1 + t_d)}\right] = \frac{\rho\delta}{1 + t_d}\left(\alpha + \frac{L_d m_d}{C_i}\right)$$

Therefore,

$$\gamma = \frac{\rho\delta L_d C_i\left(a + \dfrac{M_d}{C_i}\right)}{w^*(1 + t_d)\left[(\rho + 1) - \dfrac{t_d L_d}{1 + t_d}\right]} \qquad \ldots\ldots\ldots (B9)$$

Now $\Delta U = U_d \Delta C_d + U_i \Delta C_i$. But

$$\Delta C_i = -\gamma(m_d + w^*) + \frac{\delta L_d m_d}{1 + t_d}$$

and

$$\Delta C_a = g'(m_a)\Delta M_a + [g(m_a) - m_a g'(m_a)]\Delta L_a$$

$$= g'(m_a)\left[\gamma m_a - \frac{\delta L_a m_a}{1 + t_a}\right] + \gamma[g(m_a) - m_a g'(m_a)]$$

$$= \gamma g(m_a) - \frac{\delta L_a m_a g'(m_a)}{1 + t_a}$$

Therefore,

$$\Delta U = U_a\left[\gamma g(m_a) - \frac{\delta L_a m_a g'(m_a)}{1 + t_a}\right] + U_i\left[-\gamma(m_a + w^*) + \frac{\delta L_a m_a}{1 + t_a}\right]$$

$$= \gamma[U_a g(m_a) - U_i(m_a + w^*)] + \frac{\delta L_a m_a}{1 + t_a}[U_i - U_a g'(m_a)]$$

But as $U_i/U_a = g'(m_a)$, the second term above is zero. Hence,

$$\Delta U = \gamma U_a g'(m_a)\left[\frac{g(m_a) - m_a g'(m_a)}{g'(m_a)} - w^*\right]$$

$$= \gamma U_a g'(m_a)\left(\frac{w^*}{1 + t_a} - w^*\right)$$

$$= -\frac{t_a \gamma U_a w^* g'(m_a)}{1 + t_a}\quad\dots\dots\dots\dots\dots\dots\dots\text{(B10)}$$

Thus, ΔU is the positive if γ is negative. If $\rho > 0$, we know from (B9) that γ is negative if δ is negative, for $(a + 1)$ is larger than $t_a L_a/(1 + t_a)$, the latter term being less than unity. We can raise welfare by lowering t_a and raising t_i; thus, $t_a = t_i$ could not have been optimal.

REFERENCES

1. Bhagwati, J., 'The Pure Theory of International Trade: A Survey', *Economic Journal*, Vol. LXXIV, No. 293, March 1964, pp. 1–84.
2. Cooper, C. A. and Massell, B. F., 'Toward a General Theory of Customs Unions of Developing Countries', *Journal of Political Economy*, Vol. LXXIII, No. 5, October, pp. 461–76.
3. Corden, W. M., 'Tariffs, Subsidies and the Terms of Trade,' *Economica*, Vol. XXIV, No. 3, August 1957, pp. 235–42.
4. Johnson, H. G., 'Optimum Welfare and Maximum Revenue Tariffs', *Review of Economic Studies*, Vol. XIX, No. 48, 1951–2, pp. 28–35.
5. Johnson, H. G., 'The Cost of Protection and the Scientific Tariff', *Journal of Political Economy*, Vol. LXVIII, No. 4, August 1960, pp. 327–45.

6. Johnson, H. G., 'Tariffs and Economic Development: Some Theoretical Issues', *Journal of Development Studies*, Vol. I, No. 1, October 1964, pp. 3–30.
7. Johnson, H. G., 'Optimal Trade Intervention in the Presence of Domestic Distortions', in R. E. Caves, H. G. Johnson and P. B. Kenen (eds), *Trade Growth and the Balance of Payments: Essays in Honor of Gottfried Haberler*, Chicago, Rand McNally & Co., 1965.
8. Kemp, M. C., *The Pure Theory of International Trade*, Englewood Cliffs, N. J., Prentice-Hall, Inc., 1964.
9. Kindleberger, C. P., *International Economics*, 3rd ed., Homewood, Ill., Richard D. Irwin, Inc., 1963.
10. Meade, J. E., *Trade and Welfare*, London, Oxford University Press, 1955.

5. Tariff Structure and Resource Allocation in the Presence of Factor Substitution[1]

W. M. Corden ([1], [2]) illuminated understanding of the effects of a tariff when intermediate goods are traded by developing the concept of the effective protective rate. Unlike the nominal protective rate, the effective protective rate takes account of tariffs not only on the final good, but also on the imported inputs used in its production. Corden ([2], p. 222) defined the concept as follows: 'The effective protective rate is the percentage increase in value added *per* unit in an economic activity which is made possible by the tariff structure relative to the situation in the absence of tariffs but with the same exchange rate.' He showed, as did H. G. Johnson [4] that if the physical coefficients relating imported intermediate goods and outputs are fixed, a tariff will pull domestic resources towards activities enjoying relatively high effective protective rates.

Given the assumption of non-substitutability between imported inputs and domestic factors, one can conceive of the domestic factors as producing a value-added good in each activity, which is combined in fixed proportions with imported inputs in the manufacture of the final good. The relative prices of value-added goods will then depend on the structure of effective protective rates. The effective protective rate for an activity determines the price of its value-added good in precisely the same manner that the nominal tariff rate determines the price of a final good when intermediate goods are not traded. It follows directly from the celebrated Stolper–Samuelson theorem (Stolper and Samuelson, [8]) that, if there are two activities, the levy of a tariff will pull resources towards the activity enjoying the higher effective protective rate. If there are

[1] Jagdish Bhagwati, W. M. Corden, H. G. Johnson, J. Clark Leith and Richard Portes provided useful comments.

54

more than two activities but the number of final goods and the number of domestic factors are equal, and constant returns to scale prevail in each activity, we can conclude that a tariff will pull resources towards the activities enjoying relatively high effective protective rates; for on these assumptions the transformation surface of the value-added goods is concave, and the output mix and resource allocation depend on the effective tariff structure alone. Note that the number of imported inputs used in each activity is of no consequence given the fixed coefficients assumption.

When substitution between imported inputs and domestic factors is allowed for, alternative definitions of an effective protective rate are possible, depending on the technology used to evaluate it. Corden [3] has provided an ingenious measure of effective protective rates which can predict resource movement given a special assumption regarding the nature of substitution. Assume that substitution effects are unbiased, in the following sense. When two domestic factors and an imported input are used to make a final good, the quantity of the imported input used *per* unit of output depends only on the price ratio of the imported input and the final good; and the relative quantities used of the two domestic factors depend only on the ratio of their prices. On these assumptions, we can legitimately conceive of domestic factors as combining to produce value-added goods, which in turn combine with imported inputs to make the final goods. Now define the effective protective rate on an activity as being the proportionate increase in the price of a value-added good resulting from the levy of a tariff. Then we are back in the Stolper–Samuelson world; we can assert that a tariff will pull resources towards activities enjoying relatively high effective protective rate.

Corden has made a valuable analytical contribution in showing that effective protective rate theory is valid on some assumptions, even in the presence of substitution. But there is no reason why substitution should take this particular form. even granted that substitution effects are of this kind, effective protective rates as defined by Corden have no predictive value in practice. The technologies to be utilized in computation cannot be determined unless all production functions are known. We do not in fact know the forms of all production functions for any economy; and, if we did, we need not trouble to compute effective protective rates, for we can instead solve directly for the output mix and resource allocation entailed by a tariff. Corden has no doubt shown that the effective protective rate for an activity on his [3] definition will lie between the effective protective rates computed on the basis of free trade and post-tariff technologies. It is however possible, as Corden himself appreciates, for one activity to have a higher effective protective rate than another activity on the basis of both free trade and post-tariff technologies, but a lower effective protective rate on the Corden [3] basis. So the Corden [3] measure cannot be applied even if both the free trade and post-tariff technologies and prices are known. It is not useful for predicting resource movement when substitution effects are significant, even if these effects are unbiased in Corden's sense.

The Corden [3] definition of an effective protective rate is based on a very special assumption regarding the nature of substitution. Our purpose in this paper is to show by counter-example that, if substitution effects are biased, there cannot exist any definition of an effective protective rate, based on prices of imported inputs and outputs and on technical coefficients alone, that can be used to predict the resource movements resulting from a tariff.[1]

We now set out our counter-example. We show that, with effective protective rates on any definition whatsoever held constant, a tariff will pull resources and output in one direction on one assumption regarding the overall resource endowment, and in the opposite direction on another assumption with regard to the overall resource

---

[1] Corden said in his 1966 paper that effective protective rates measured on the basis of free trade technology would predict resource movement in the presence of substitution. Tan [9] showed, in a brilliant doctoral dissertation submitted to Stanford University, that nothing can be said in general regarding the effects of effective protective rates so defined on resource allocation. He did not, however, provide a counter-example.

Another possible definition of an effective protective rate is the difference between the ratio of domestic value-added in the post-tariff and free trade situations on the one hand and unity on the other. Travis [10] and Naya and Anderson [6] have used this definition. We show later that the effective protective rate so defined may not lie between the effective protective rates computed with free trade and post-tariff technologies.

We have devised simple counter-examples to both the above measures of effective protective rates. These are not, however, reproduced, as the counter-example that follows in the text above invalidates any measure whatsoever.

Leith [5] provides a valuable analysis of substitution, but concludes that 'the effective protection rate remains the indicator of resource allocation (together with the elasticity of supply of value added) . . .' (p. 594). When substitution is biased, the concept of a value-added good which has a supply elasticity is illegitimate.

endowment. We assume that two domestic factors, land and labour, and an important input, metal, are used in each of the two activities in an economy. Both domestic factors are always fully employed. World prices of metal and of the two outputs are fixed, and are normalized at unity. In each of the two activities, constant returns to scale prevail and production function is concave.

We write:

(1) x_i, y_i for the metal–labour and land–labour ratios in activity i, $i = 1, 2$.

(2) L_1 for the amount of labour used in activity 1, the economy's total supply of labour being normalized at unity.

(3) y for the total amount of land in the economy.

(4) t for the *ad valorem* rate of subsidy on import of metal. Both outputs are always free of tax or subsidy.

(5) f^i for output *per* unit of labour in activity i, $1 = 1, 2$.

The two production functions are:

$$f^1 = [0.75 + 0.25\, x_1^{-10}]^{-.01}\, y_1^{0.9} \tag{1}$$

$$f^2 = x_2^{0.20}\, y_1^{0.65} \tag{2}$$

With these production functions, the equations determining equilibrium input ratios are as follows:

$$0.025\,[0.75 + 0.25 x_1^{-10}]^{-1.01}\, x_1^{-11}\, y_1^{0.9} = 1 - t \tag{3}$$

$$0.20\, x_2^{-0.8}\, y_2^{0.65} \qquad\qquad\quad = 1 - t \tag{4}$$

$$0.9\,[0.75 + 0.25 x_1^{-10}]^{-.01}\, y_1^{-0.1} = 0.65\, x_2{}^{0.20}\, y_2^{-0.35} \tag{5}$$

$$0.075\,[0.75 + 0.25\, x_1^{-10}]^{-1.01}\, y_1^{0.9} = {}^{0.16}\, x_2^{0.20}\, y_2^{0.65} \tag{6}$$

Equations (3) and (4) state that the marginal value product of metal in each activity equals its subsidy-inclusive price of $1 - t$. Equation (5) states that the marginal value product of land is the same in each activity. Equation (6) states that the marginal value product of labour is the same in each activity.

Once a subsidy rate t is specified, equations (3) to (6) can be solved to obtain the equilibrium values of x_1, y_1, x_2 and y_2. The factor allocations between activities are then determined from:

$$L_1\, y_1 + (1 - L_1)\, y_2 = y \tag{7}$$

Given y, this equation determines L_1, the amount of labour devoted to activity 1 (the amount of labour devoted to activity 2 will then be $1 - L_1$), and $L_1 y_1$ and $(1 - L_1)\, y_2$, the amounts of land devoted to activities 1 and 2 respectively.

We specified valued 0 and 0·2 for t and 0·10 and 5.00 for y. The solutions[1] for equilibrium factor ratios are listed in Table 1.

TABLE 1

Variable	Activity 1		Activity 2	
	$t = 0$	$t = 0·2$	$t = 0$	$t = 0·2$
x	0·6065	0·6301	0·0163	0·0248
y	7·8986	6·4787	0·0753	0·0895

The solutions for factor allocations depend also on the aggregate land availability. These are listed in Table 2.

TABLE 2

Total Land Available	Factor Allocation	Activity 1		Activity 2	
		$t = 0$	$t = 0·2$	$t = 0$	$t = 0·2$
0·10	Metal	0·001915	0·001035	0·016249	0·024759
5·00	Metal	0·381786	0·484271	0·006039	0·005740
0·10	Labour	0·003157	0·001643	0·996844	0·998357
	Land	0·024938	0·010647	0·750620	0·089353
5·00	Labour	0·629491	0·768562	0·370509	0·231438
	Land	4·972101	4·979286	0·027899	0·020714

It is obvious from Table 2 that the imposition of the same subsidy rate of 20 per cent *ad valorem* on metal shifts *both* labour and land from activity 1 to activity 2 (as compared to the free trade position) when total land available is 0·10 units, while labour and land move in the opposite direction, i.e., from activity 2 to activity 1 (as compared to the free trade position) when total land available is 5·00 units. This conclusively shows that an effective protective rate howsoever defined on the basis of technical coefficients and prices of imported inputs and outputs cannot predict resource movement independently of the overall resource endowment, given our assumptions regarding the nature of substitution effects.

[1] We are grateful to Professor Kirit S. Parikh of the Indian Statistical Institute for solving equations (3)–(6) on the IBM 1620 computer of the Indian Planning Commission.

Note further that the direction of change of the relative outputs of the two goods resulting from grant of the subsidy will be different, on the alternative assumptions regarding the factor endowment. When the total land supply is 0·10 units, the subsidy not only shift land and labour to activity 2, but also results in less (more) use of metal in activity 1 (2). So output of activity 1 declines and that of activity 2 rises. On the other hand, when the total land supply is 5·0 units, the subsidy moves land and labour from activity 2 to activity 1, and results in less (more) use of metal in activity 2 (1). Hence in this latter case output of activity 2 declines and that of activity 1 increases.[1]

Why is the overall resource endowment of significance? The answer is that, when a subsidy is granted, the marginal conditions for optimality entail that the land-labour ratios move in *opposite* directions in the two activities. So the allocations of land and labour between the activities consistent with full employment of both factors depend on the resource endowment. Factor proportions cannot change in opposite directions in the two activities if intermediate goods are not traded and a tariff is levied on a final good; for then the ratios of the marginal physical products of the factors cannot be equal in the two activities in both the free trade and post-tariff situations. That is why the Stolper–Samuelson result holds without reference to the factor endowment. But when intermediate goods are traded, domestic factor proportions can change in opposite directions, as in our counter-example. Note that a *reversal* of domestic factor-intensities does not take place.

We have shown that when biased substitution takes place effective protective rates on any definition cannot predict resource movement; and that, when substitution is unbiased, effective protective rates defined so as to indicate resource shifts are either redundant or

---

[1] We have computed the values of the effective protective rates on the basis of free trade and post-tariff technologies, and of a 'true' effective protective rate defined as the difference between the ratio of domestic value-added in the post-tariff and free trade situations on the one hand and unity on the other. These are as follows:

Activity	'True' EPR	FTEPR	PTEPR
1	0·0011	0·0275	0·0217
2	0·0000	0·0667	0·0500

It is of interest to note that the 'true' effective protective rate for either activity does not lie between those evaluated with free trade and post-tariff technologies.

cannot be computed. But how important is substitution? If it is not, as Corden [3] holds, effective protective rate theory would still be useful. A number of instances come readily to mind in which substitution between domestic factors and intermediate goods would appear to be of significance in the real world. Thus fertilizers are in general a good substitute for land, and so are pesticides. The quantities of imported pulp used to make a ton of paper or of imported iron ore used to make a ton of steel will depend in part on the economics of collecting waste paper or scrap for re-use; in poor countries with low wage rates relatively more labour is likely to be applied to such purposes. The output of steel from a blast furnace can be raised by injecting increased quantities of imported petroleum products.

Even when, with any given process, the quantities of imported inputs used *per* unit of output are invariant with respect to changes in tariff rates, the levy of a tariff can result in a switch of processes that entails substitution. Thus the import of liquid ammonia instead of crude petroleum to make fertilizers may save capital relatively more than labour.

In engineering industries, the various components combined to make a given product may always be the same. But the levy of a tariff may result in some components hitherto domestically produced being imported, and in a shift from foreign to domestic sources of supply for other components. This process of substitution may well be biased.

Corden [2] suggested that the annual services of tradeable capital goods can be treated in the same way as imported intermediate goods, when it is legitimate to assume a perfectly elastic supply of capital funds on world markets. If then land and labour are domestic primary factors, and the annual service of equipment can be treated as an intermediate good, it is clear that there is considerable room for substitution. Earth-moving equipment substitutes for labour in construction work. The use of an automatic loom instead of a hand-loom in the weaving of cloth displaces much labour but virtually no land. The assumption that the supply of capital from abroad is perfectly elastic is, however, realistic only in exceptional cases; in general, capital must be regarded as a domestic factor of production, inelastic in supply in the short run. Changes in the supply of capital as a result of domestic savings and international capital movements are appropriately taken into account in dynamic analysis.

We must conclude that substitution effects will often be significant, and that therefore effective protective rates are likely to be a poor guide to the resource movements resulting from the levy of a tariff. This conclusion may appear nihilistic. But in our view the invalidity of effective protective rate theory is of little practical consequence. The levy of escalated tariffs may or may not pull resources towards the later stages of processing; in either case, rich countries which can raise revenue at less welfare cost in other ways should be advised to abolish all trade barriers. A less developed country may, on the other hand, sometimes be justified in levying trade taxes to collect revenue, particularly when international income transfers are inadequate. But, when this is the case, the second-best revenue tariff entailed by the economy's social welfare and production functions must be computed and levied, and the resulting effective protective rates are of no particular significance. Domestic distortions, externalities and non-economic objectives are appropriately handled through taxes and subsidies on domestic economic variables.[1] Thus in many situations the optimal policy with regard to foreign trade is non-intervention. When the levy of trade taxes is justified, the optimal tariff must be determined with reference to a specified objective; and the effective protective rates entailed by this tariff are of no relevance.

REFERENCES

1. Corden, W. M., 'The Tariff', in A. Hunter [Ed.], *The Economics of Australian Industry*, Melbourne, Melbourne University Press, 1963, pp. 162–3.
2. Corden, W. M., 'The Structure of a Tariff System and the Effective Protective Rate', *Journal of Political Economy*, Vol. LXXIV, No. 3, June 1966, pp. 221–37.
3. Corden, W. M., 'The Substitution Problem in the Theory of Effective Protection', mimeographed, 1969, a chapter in his book on *The Theory of Protection* (forthcoming).
4. Johnson, H. G., 'The Theory of Tariff Structure with Special Reference to World Trade and Development', in *Trade and Development*, Geneva, Institut Universitaire de Hautes Études Internationales, 1965, pp. 9–29.
5. Leith, J. Clark, 'Substitution and Supply Elasticities in Calculating the Effective Protective Rare'. *Quarterly Journal of Economics*, Vol. LXXXII, No. 4, November 1968, pp. 588–601.
6. Naya, S. and Anderson, J., 'Substitution and Two Concepts of Effective Rate of Protection', mimeographed, 1968, forthcoming in *American Economic Review*.

[1] Ramaswami [7] discusses the optimal policies for handling various distortions, externalities and non-economic objectives, and cites earlier papers by Bhagwati, Corden, Johnson, the present authors and others.

7. Ramaswami, V. K., 'Optimal Policies to Promote Industrialization in Less Developed Countries', mimeographed, 1969, an essay in Paul Streeten (ed.), *Essays in honour of Thomas Balogh* (forthcoming), Ch. 13 in this volume.

8. Stolper, W. F. and Samuelson, P. A., 'Protection and Real Wages', *Review of Economic Studies*, Vol. IX, November 1941, pp. 58–73. Reprinted in *Readings in the Theory of International Trade*, Philadelphia and Toronto, The Blakiston Company, 1949, pp. 333–57.

9. Tan, A., 'Differential Tariffs, Negative Value-Added and the Theory of Effective Protection', Chapter 3 of a doctoral dissertation submitted to Stanford University, mimeographed, 1968.

10. Travis, W. P., 'The Effective Rate of Protection and the Question of Labour Protection in the United States', *Journal of Political Economy*, Vol. 76, No. 3, May/June 1968, pp. 443–61.

6. Export Subsidy and Implicit Exchange Rates When Intermediate Goods are Traded[1]

Countries which sustain unrealistic exchange rates by applying import controls sometimes subsidize exports by granting import licenses against export earnings. Among the data relevant to the choice of a realistic exchange rate[2] are the implicit exchange rates confronting exporters under such systems. Yet there has been virtually no discussion in the literature of how implicit exchange rates are to be computed. When imported intermediate goods enter into export production, the implicit exchange rate for a product will in general differ from the subsidy-inclusive realization in domestic currency for exports worth one unit of foreign currency at world prices. In this paper we elucidate the relationship between export subsidy and implicit exchange rates under alternative types of subsidy schemes.

The conventional wisdom with regard to entitlement systems, as with regard to multiple exchange rates, is that uniformity is desirable. But what is meant by uniformity has not been adequately discussed. We propose to consider the means by which uniformity in implicit exchange rates can be secured under entitlement systems; on some assumptions, this may mean lack of uniformity in export subsidy rates. We do not assert that uniformity is necessarily desirable, from

---

[1] *Editorial Note;* This paper was written by Ramaswami for the forthcoming Rosenstein-Rodan *Festschrift.* It was probably intended to be revised in the light of further work: his notes included some rough drafts of work on models using more than one product and factor, for example, and he had been in correspondence with friends, including Jean Baneth, about the paper. To retain the paper in its original version, only minor editorial changes have been made.

[2] Several other types of information will be relevant to the realistic choice of policy. Mention may be made in particular of anticipated aid inflows.

E

the viewpoint of optimality of the solution, even if it is worthwhile on practical grounds because of lack of adequate information on which discrimination can be based. Usually schemes of this kind are not designed to secure second-best solutions given clear cut objectives; and therefore very little can be said about what is optimal. It is, however, worthwhile to understand what uniformity in implicit exchange rates entails.

The implicit exchange rate for the export of a product is that rate which, if all input prices confronting producers other than those of directly imported intermediate goods remain constant, will leave export profitability unchanged if the subsidy scheme is abolished. It is essentially a partial equilibrium concept. Of course, many prices will change if the exchange rate is altered, and the computation of an equilibrium exchange rate in principle requires general equilibrium analysis. Reform of the tariff and import control structure which may accompany the change in the exchange rate would have to be taken into account in such general equilibrium analysis. Nevertheless, study of the array of implicit exchange rates under subsidy schemes is of interest.

Our procedure is to consider, for our formal analysis, a simple model in which only one good is produced and is partly exported and partly consumed at home. The production of this good requires the use of the sole domestic factor, labour, and wholly imported metal. An imported consumer good also enters into consumption. Production is under conditions of constant returns to scale. We initially assume that the metal-labour ratio is fixed, and thereafter turn to the case in which there is substitution between metal and labour, on the basis of diminishing returns to varying factor proportions. The country has no national monopoly power, and therefore world prices of tradeables are fixed; we normalize these at unity. We assume that the supply of labour is perfectly elastic at some fixed wage rate. The utility function is well-behaved. The optimal devaluation is defined as the proportionate increase in the domestic price of a unit of foreign currency needed to make exporting profitable without subsidies. In this simple model, the implicit exchange rate is simply the optimal exchange rate that will secure this result. We assume that either trade is balanced, or that there is a given quantum of aid inflow which is invariable with respect to the trade policy followed.

We compare an initial situation in which exporting is worthwhile given the exchange rate and the wage rate, with a later situation in which the wage rate has risen because of inflation. In this second situation the formal exchange rate is unchanged but exports are subsidized.

I

We consider first the fixed coefficients case. Assume that fixed amounts i of metal and L of labour are needed to make one unit of the domestically produced good. If the domestic price of a unit of foreign currency is e, the wage rate under free trade must be $e(1 - i)/L = w^*$.

Suppose, however, that as a result of inflation the wage rate is rigid at a level $w = aw^*$ where $a > 1$. A devaluation such that e changes to $e' = ea$, floating of the exchange rate, or levy of a uniform tax on imports and subsidy on exports at the rate $(a - 1)$ or $(w - w^*)/w^*$ would secure free trade first-best at the higher wage rate.

But suppose that the government, while willing to accept partial *de facto* devaluation, wishes to supply some quantities of the imported consumer good to consumers and/or of metal to producers at the price 'e''. It therefore requires exporters to surrender part of the export proceeds at the official exchange rate, while permitting them to retain a fraction 'r' of these proceeds to import directly either the consumer good or metal.

Model One

Suppose initially that the ration of metal provided to producers at the official exchange rate 'e' is less than full employment requirements, and that 'r' is larger than the metal content 'i' of the domestically produced good. Let p_r be the domestic price of the right to import goods worth unity abroad against export sales, and let p_d be the domestic price of the domestically produced good. As unit cost must equal the domestic price, we have

$$p_d = Lw + i(e + p_r) \quad \dots\dots\dots\dots\dots\dots \quad (1)$$

The realization per unit of exports is $e + rp_r$; and a marginal condition for profit maximization is that

$$p_d = Lw + i(e + p_r) = e + rp_r \quad \dots\dots\dots\dots \quad (2)$$

65

So the export subsidy under this scheme, defined as the difference between the domestic price and the export price at the official exchange rate as a proportion of the latter price, is rp_r/e.

We wish to compare this rate of export subsidy with the optimal devaluation. The latter expression is obviously $(w - w^*)/w^*$. Now

$$Lw^* + ie = e \qquad\qquad (3)$$

From (2) and (3),

$$L(w - w^*) = p_r(r - i) \qquad\qquad (4)$$

From (3),

$$Lw^* = e(1 - i) \qquad\qquad (5)$$

So

$$\frac{w - w^*}{w^*} = \frac{p_r(r - i)}{e(1 - i)} \qquad\qquad (6)$$

Equation (6) states that the optimal devaluation equals the ratio of the market value of the right to retain foreign exchange in excess of import content of exports, as a proportion of the price at the official exchange rate of a unit of exports net of import content. Now

$$\frac{rp_r}{e} - \frac{w - w^*}{w^*} = \frac{rp_r}{e} - \frac{p_r(r - i)}{e(1 - i)}$$

$$= \frac{ipr(1 - r)}{e(1 - i)} > 0 \text{ for all } r < 1 \qquad\qquad (7)$$

Equation (7) shows that the export subsidy rate is greater than the optimal devaluation required. It would be erroneous therefore to regard the export subsidy rate as the measure of over-valuation; it is expression (6) that should be used.

Model Two

Now suppose that the government makes available the entire metal needed to meet full employment requirements, out of the foreign exchange surrendered at the official rate. The foreign exchange retained by exporters is used only to import the consumer good. In that case, the price of the domestically produced good is

$$p_d = Lw + ie \qquad\qquad (8)$$

We now have

$$p_d = Lw + ie = e + rp_r \qquad\qquad (9)$$

As

$$Lw^* + ie = e, \quad \text{...........................} \quad (10)$$

$$L(w - w^*) = rp_r \quad \text{.........................} \quad (11)$$

Now from (5) and (11),

$$\frac{w - w^*}{w^*} = \frac{rp_r}{e(1 - i)} \quad \text{........................} \quad (12)$$

Equation (12) states that in this case the optimal devaluation equals the ratio of the right to retain foreign exchange *without deducting the import content of exports*, as a proportion of the price at the official exchange rate of a unit of exports net of import content.

Note that in this case the export subsidy rate is *lower* than the optimal devaluation. We have

$$\frac{rp_r}{e} - \frac{w - w^*}{w^*} = \frac{rp_r}{e} - \frac{irp_r}{e(1 - i)} < 0 \quad \text{...............}(13)$$

In both cases the domestic price of the imported consumer good is, of course, $e(1 + p_r)$.

Even at this early stage of the analysis a reference to the real world may be in order. In pre-devaluation India, manufacturers were by and large short of imported inputs, and the market prices of these inputs reflected the premia on import entitlement licenses. In Pakistan, on the other hand, raw materials were often available in adequate quantities at the official exchange rate, and bonus vouchers were used to import consumer goods. This suggests that export subsidy rates over-stated in pre-devaluation India, and for several periods under-stated in Pakistan, the extent of over-valuation of the currency.

II

We now introduce tariffs into the analysis, while continuing to assume fixed coefficients. Suppose that the duty rates on metal and the imported consumer good are t_m and t_i respectively. Duty drawback is granted on the import content of exports.

Model Three
Consider first the case in which metal supplies at the official exchange

67

rate are less than full employment requirements. When there is balance with a wage rate of w^*, the domestic price of the good made at home is

$$p_d = w^*L + ie(1 + t_m) = e + iet_m \qquad \ldots\ldots\ldots\ldots(14)$$

and drawback per unit of exports is iet_m.

Under the subsidy scheme,

$$p_d = Lw + i(e + p_r) + iet_m \qquad \ldots\ldots\ldots\ldots\ldots(15)$$

In equilibrium, the RHS of (15) must equal total proceeds per unit of exports, which now include drawback; so

$$p_d = Lw + i(e + p_r) + iet_m = e + rp_r + iet_m \qquad \ldots\ldots(16)$$

Hence the export subsidy rate defined as the difference between the domestic price and the export price at the official exchange rate, as a proportion of the latter, is now $(rp_r + iet_m)/e$. It is readily verified from (14) and (16) that expression (6) still holds; once more therefore:

$$\frac{w - w^*}{w^*} = \frac{p_r(r - i)}{e(1 - i)} \qquad \ldots\ldots\ldots\ldots\ldots\ldots(6)$$

As $(rp_r + iet_m)/e > rp_r/e$, our conclusion that the export subsidy rate overstates the optimal extent of devaluation still holds. [The tariff on the imported consumer good merely has the result of making its market price $e(1 + p_r + t_i)$.]

Model Four

Consider now the case in which metal supplied at the official exchange rate suffices to meet full employment requirements. It is readily verified that expression (12) still holds;

$$\frac{w - w^*}{w^*} = \frac{rp_r}{e(1 - i)} \qquad \ldots\ldots\ldots\ldots\ldots(12)$$

Compare the export subsidy rate $(rp_r + iet_m)/e$ with this expression. We have

$$\frac{rp_r + iet_m}{e} - \frac{rp_r}{e(1 - i)} = -\frac{irp_r}{e(1 - i)} + it_m \qquad \ldots\ldots(17)$$

This expression (17) $>/< 0$ depending on whether $rp_r/[e(1 - i)] >/< t_m$; no general conclusion can be drawn.

III

We now introduce substitution. In order to avoid tiresome algebra, we assume that no tariffs are levied; the analysis can readily be extended to cover tariffs. We consider four cases: (1) The ration of metal is less than full employment requirements, and there is no preferential treatment with respect to metal needed for export production. (2) The ration of metal is less than full employment requirements. Exporters are allowed additionally to import the metal actually used in export production, plus metal or the consumer good worth a specified fraction of exports, at the official rate. (3) We next consider the special case of (2) in which the free trade technique is maintained in export production. (4) The ration of metal covers full employment requirements, and a specified fraction of export earnings can be used to import the consumer good.

Model Five
We assume that the ration of metal is less than full employment requirements. Exporters can use a fraction 'r' of earnings to import metal or the consumer good. There is no privileged treatment for metal used for export production; and the same technology will be used in production for the home market and for export. We write L, i and L', i' for the input cofficients in the first-best and disequilibrium situations respectively.
We now have

$$Lw^* + ie = e \quad \dots\dots\dots\dots\dots\dots\dots\dots\dots\dots\dots\dots(18)$$

$$L'w + i'(e + p_r) = e + rp_r = p_d \quad \dots\dots\dots\dots\dots(19)$$

As use of input coefficients other than those which minimize costs for given factor prices results in higher unit cost,

$$L'w^* + i'e > e \quad \dots\dots\dots\dots\dots\dots\dots\dots\dots\dots\dots\dots(20)$$

$$Lw + i(e + p_z) > e + rp_r \quad \dots\dots\dots\dots\dots\dots\dots\dots(21)$$

From (18) and (21),

$$L(w - w^*) > p_r(r - i)$$

From (18),

$$Lw^* = e(1 - i)$$

So

$$\frac{w - w^*}{w^*} > \frac{p_r(r - i)}{1 - i}$$

From (19) and (20),

$$L'(w - w^*) < p_r(r - i')$$

From (20),

$$L'w^* > e(1 - i')$$

So

$$\frac{w - w^*}{w^*} < \frac{p_r(r - i')}{e(1 - i')}$$

Thus

$$\frac{p_r(r - i')}{e(1 - i')} > \frac{w - w^*}{w^*} > \frac{p_r(r - i)}{e(1 - i)} \quad \dots\dots\dots\dots(22)$$

We see from (22) that the market value of the right to retain foreign exchange in excess of the import content of exports in the post-subsidy situation, as a proportion of the price at the official exchange rate of a unit of exports net of post-subsidy import content, is *greater* than the optimal devaluation.

It is then readily verified that the export subsidy rate exceeds the optimal devaluation. Given (22), we need only show that

$$\frac{rp_r}{e} - \frac{p_r(r - i')}{e(1 - i')} > 0$$

We have:

$$\frac{rp_r}{e} - \frac{p_r(r - i')}{e(1 - i')} = \frac{rp_r - i'rp_r - rp_r + i'p_r}{e(1 - i')} = \frac{i'p_r(1 - r)}{e(1 - i')} > 0 . \quad (23)$$

Model Six

We now assume that exporters get a metal ration less than full employment requirements, and that they are permitted additionally to import at the official rate both (a) the actual import content of exports, and (b) metal for home use and/or the imported consumer good worth a specified fraction of export earnings. The technique in export production will now be more metal-intensive than in production for home use, We write $L, i; L', i'$; and $L''; i''$ for input coefficients in first-best, post-subsidy export production and post-subsidy production for the home market. We now have

$$Lw^* + ie = e \quad \dots\dots\dots\dots\dots\dots\dots(24)$$

$$L'w + i'e = e + r'p_r \quad \dots\dots\dots\dots(25)$$

$$L''w + i''(e + p_r) = p_d \quad \dots\dots\dots\dots\dots (26)$$

$$L'w* + i'e > e \quad \dots\dots\dots\dots\dots\dots (27)$$

$$Lw + ie > e + r'p_r \quad \dots\dots\dots\dots\dots (28)$$

From (25) and (27),

$$L'(w - w*) < r'p_r$$

From (27), $L'w* > e(1 - i')$

So

$$\frac{w - w*}{w*} < \frac{r'p_r}{e(1 - i')}$$

From (24) and (28),

$$L(w - w*) > r'p_r$$

From (24),

$$Lw* = e(1 - i)$$

So

$$\frac{w - w*}{w*} > \frac{r'p_r}{e(1 - i)}$$

Thus

$$\frac{r'p_r}{(e1 - i')} > \frac{w - w*}{w*} > \frac{r'p_r}{e(1 - i)} \quad \dots\dots\dots\dots (29)$$

In this model, it is necessary to distinguish between two alternative definitions of the export subsidy rate: (a) the premium earned on the entitlement per unit of exports as a proportion of the export price, and the difference between the domestic and the export price as a proportion of the latter.

We first show that the subsidy rate on definition (a) exceeds the optimal devaluation. In view of (29), it suffices to show that

$$\frac{(i' + r')p_r}{e} - \frac{r'p_r}{e(1 - i')} = \frac{p_r[i + r' - i'^2 - i'r' - r']}{e(1 - i')}$$

$$= \frac{i'p_r[1 - i' - r']}{e(1 - i')} > 0 \quad \dots\dots\dots\dots (30)$$

by assumption that some part of export proceeds is surrendered to government.

We next show that the export subsidy rate on definition (a) is higher than that on definition (b). From (25),

$$e + (i' + r')p_r = L'w + i'(e + p_r)$$

Now

$$L'w + i'(e + p_r) > L''w + i''(e + p_r) = p_d$$

So

$$e + (i' + r')p_r > p_d,$$

or

$$\frac{(i' + r')p_r}{e} > \frac{p_d - e}{e} \quad \dots\dots\dots\dots\dots\dots\dots\dots(31)$$

Finally we show that the export subsidy rate on definition (b) exceeds the optimal devaluation.
We have:

$$L''w^* + i''e > e \quad \dots\dots\dots\dots\dots\dots\dots\dots\dots\dots\dots(32)$$

$$L''w \; + i''(e + p_r) = p_d \quad \dots\dots\dots\dots\dots \text{ from (26)}$$

So

$$L''(w - w^*) < p_d - e - i''p_r$$
$$L''w^* > e(1 - i'')$$

So

$$\frac{w - w^*}{w^*} < \frac{p_d - e - i''p_r}{e(1 - i'')} \quad \dots\dots\dots\dots\dots\dots\dots(33)$$

Now

$$\frac{p_d - e}{e} - \frac{p_d - e - i''p_r}{e(1 - i'')}$$

$$= \frac{p_d - e - i''p_d + i''e - p_d + e + i''p_r}{e(1 - i'')}$$

$$= \frac{i''(e + p_r - p_d)}{e(1 - i'')} \quad \dots\dots\dots\dots\dots\dots\dots\dots\dots\dots(34)$$

But

$$L'w + i'(e + p_r) > p_d \quad \dots\dots\dots\dots\dots \text{ from (26)}$$
$$\text{and } L'w + i'e = e + r'p_r \quad \dots\dots\dots\dots \text{ from (25)}$$

So

$$e + r'p_r - p_d > - i'p_r,$$

or
$$e + p_r - p_a > - i'p_r + p_r - r'p_r,$$

or
$$e + p_r - p_a > p_r(1 - i' - r') > 0 \quad \ldots\ldots\ldots\ldots(35)$$

From (33), (34) and (35), we conclude that

$$\frac{p_a - e}{e} > \frac{w - w^*}{w^*} \quad \ldots\ldots\ldots\ldots\ldots\ldots\ldots\ldots(36)$$

Model Seven

It is of some interest to consider how, on Model Six assumptions, free trade technology can be maintained in export production. The proportionate increases in the price of metal for export production and the realization per unit of exports must equal the proportionate rise in the wage rate above the first-best level. We must have

$$Lw^* + ie = e, \quad \ldots\ldots\ldots\ldots\ldots\ldots(37)$$

$$Lw + i\left(\frac{ew}{w^*}\right) = e\left(\frac{w}{w^*}\right) \quad \ldots\ldots\ldots\ldots(38)$$

So we must have $e' = ew/w^*$ and $e + r'p_r = ew/w^*$. If $e + r'p_r = ew/w^*$, we have $p_r = e(w - w^*)/r'w^*$. To secure this, r' has to be chosen.

Let the fraction of the actual import content in export production which exporters can secure at the price 'e' be 'f'. They have to buy the rest of the import content of exports at the market rate. Then we must so choose 'f' that

$$fe + (1 - f)\left[e + \frac{e(w - w^*)}{r'w^*}\right] = \frac{ew}{w^*}$$

$$\therefore f\left[e - e - \frac{e(w - w^*)}{r'w^*}\right] = \frac{ew}{w^*} - e - \frac{e(w - w^*)}{r'w^*}$$

$$= \frac{er'w - er'w^* - ew + ew^*}{r'w^*}$$

So

$$f = \frac{r'w^* + w - w^* - r'w}{w - w^*} = 1 - r' \quad \ldots\ldots\ldots\ldots(39)$$

This solution implies that there is a uniform premium on the right to import metal for home use and the consumer good. Therefore the amount of foreign exchange secured by government is determined. It would, however, be possible to secure different premia for the right to import metal for home use on the one hand and the consumer good on the other by specifying the proportions in which 'f' should be divided between these uses. The larger the share of metal for home use relative to that of the consumer good, the lower will be the production cost and the greater the consumption cost of the entitlement scheme. The difference between the value at market prices and at the official rate of allocations of metal and/or the imported consumer good can be regarded as a subsidy to recipients. One can establish equivalance between a scheme of this kind and levy of the second-best revenue tariff to secure specified revenues for re-distribution to consumers. As Srinivasan and the present author [1] have shown, such a second-best tariff would be characterized by maintenance of the free trade technique in production for export, and in general by different tax rates on metal for home use and the imported consumer good.

Model Eight
We now assume that the metal ration suffices to meet full employment requirements. The entitlement is used to import the consumer good; thus

$$L'w + ie = e \qquad \dots\dots\dots\dots\dots\dots\dots (40)$$

$$L' + i'e = e + r'p_r = p_d \qquad \dots\dots\dots\dots\dots (41)$$

Inequality (29) of Case 2 holds.

The export subsidy rate, howsoever defined, is $r'p_r/e$. This is *lower* than the optimal devaluation $(w - w^*)/w^*$. Given (29), we need only show that

$$\frac{r'p_r}{e} - \frac{r'p_r}{e(1-i)} = \frac{r'p - ir'p_r - r'p_r}{e(1-i)} < 0 \qquad \dots\dots\dots (42)$$

IV

In a multi-factor and multi-product world, the relationships between export subsidy rates, implicit exchange rates and the optimal rate change are complex. It is clear, however, that when raw material allocations do not cover full requirements, the premium on the entitlement net of import content as a fraction of the export price is a better measure of an implicit exchange rate than the export subsidy rate. It is further of interest to note that whereas when material allocations at the official rate are inadequate the export subsidy rate overstates the rate change required, the opposite is the case when entitlements are used solely to import consumer goods. The reason for this divergence is that, whereas in the former case a rate change accompanied by liberalization *reduces* the effective prices of imported inputs, these effective prices *rise* in the latter case.

When raw material allocations at the official rate are not sufficient to meet full employment requirements, uniformity in implicit exchange rates is most likely to be secured by a scheme under which exporters receive part of their entitlement based on the import content of exports and the remainder at a flat percentage of the f.o.b. realization. We have shown, if the free trade technique is to be maintained in production for export, the entitlement based on import content of exports will be somewhat less than import content; given the fact that prices of domestic inputs are higher than is consistent with the current exchange rate in the absence of export subsidies, technique in export production would be unduly import-intensive if full import content were allowed. Thus divergence in export subsidy rates would be entailed by a policy of uniformity in implicit exchange rates. When material allocations suffice to meet full employment requirements, for example because of large aid inflows, one cannot use the device of variation in materials entitlements to discriminate between commodities. Technology in all production in the economy would be unduly import intensive. Uniformity in implicit exchange rates would be secured by adjusting entitlement rates so that profits on sale of the entitlement (without deducting import content) on a unit of exports, as a proportion of the price net of import content, is the same for all exportables. Such uniformity is, however, not necessarily optimal; all techniques will be based on unduly low relative prices of imported inputs, and welfare can obviously be raised by a rate change combined with levy of optimal taxes to secure any income redistribution that is desired.

REFERENCES

[1] Ramaswami, V. K. and T. N. Srinivasan, 'Optimal Subsidies and Taxes when Some Factors are Traded', *Journal of Political Economy*, Vol. 76, August 1968, pp. 569–82. This constitutes chapter 4 of the present volume.

7. The Effects of Accumulation on the Terms of Trade[1]

The effects of the process of accumulation (as distinguished from those of completed accumulation) on the terms of trade are analysed in this paper. The analytical device employed is to regard a rise in the rate of accumulation as a shift of demand from consumer goods to capital goods at constant prices. The effects of completed accumulation on the terms of trade if accumulation continues at a steady rate are also considered.

Model One

Assumptions: Two countries (Mancunia and Agraria), two products (engineering products and food), two factors (capital and labour), constant returns to scale in engineering, diminishing returns to scale in agriculture, production of both commodities in both countries, a higher capital–labour ratio in engineering than in agriculture at all product price ratios, given production functions and no 'inferior' product in consumption.

We suppose that engineering products can be used both for consumption and as capital goods, while food is only a consumer good.

Initially there is equilibrium in production, consumption and trade with no investment in either country; engineering products are used only as consumer goods.

It is assumed that Mancunia's exportables are engineering products, while Agraria exports food.

The citizens of Mancunia now decide to raise their stock of capital by installing part of the output of engineering products in new factories. If at the same time they reduce their use of engineering products for consumption by an equal amount without requiring any

[1] I am indebted to Mr T. Balogh, Mr J. Black, Mr P. P. Streeten and Mr J. Bhagwati for comments on a first draft.

change in the relative prices of engineering products and food to induce them to do so, the terms of trade will be unchanged.

It is, however, unlikely that Mancunians will reduce their consumption of engineering products alone at unchanged prices, to finance the investment they wish to undertake. It is reasonable to suppose that the cut in consumption will be divided between the two consumer goods, if prices remain the same. But if the reduction in the quantity of engineering products used for consumption in Mancunia is less than the quantity of these products diverted to investment, there must be a fall in the volume of engineering products offered to Agraria at constant prices. The terms of trade of Mancunia will improve, the change in relative prices resulting in increased output of engineering products and reduced use of these products for consumption in both countries.

Conversely, an attempt by the citizens of Agraria to raise their stock of capital must worsen that country's terms of trade, unless the reduction of consumption required to finance the investment is confined to engineering goods.

After the process of accumulation has been completed the terms of trade will be less favourable to Mancunia than in the initial situation Professor Johnson has developed this point in [1] his argument being on the following lines. Suppose the product price ratio to remain the same after accumulation has taken place in (say) Mancunia. As the product price ratio is unchanged, factor proportions must be the same as before in each use. But this must mean a reduced output of the labour-intensive product, for an increased stock of capital can be employed with a given labour force and unchanged techniques only by a transfer of labour to the capital-intensive use. If the labour-intensive product is not an 'inferior' good in consumption its relative price must rise. The labour-intensive product being Mancunia's importable, Agraria's terms of trade must improve.

As accumulation proceeds, the level of food output in the two countries taken together at any given product price ratio will fall steadily. Mancunia's terms of trade must therefore deteriorate and those of Agraria improve. But this trend may be slowed down or even reversed for a time as a result of increased levels of investment in either country.

Model Two
Assumptions: Two countries (Mancunia and Agraria), two pro-

ducts (engineering products and food), two factors (capital and labour), constant or diminishing returns to scale in both engineering and agriculture, specialization by Mancunia in engineering and by Agraria in agriculture, and no 'inferior' product in consumption.

We suppose once more that engineering products can be used both as capital goods and as consumer goods, while food is used for consumption alone.

The effect of completed accumulation in Mancunia while Agraria remains stationary is to worsen Mancunia's terms of trade, as has has been shown by Professor Johnson.[2] For, by assumption of the absence of 'inferior' goods, the citizens of Mancunia will want more importables at constant prices. Similarly, completed accumulation in Agraria will worsen that country's terms of trade if Mancunia has remained stationary.

The process of accumulation must improve Mancunia's terms of trade and worsen those of Agraria. For, at constant prices, Mancunia will offer less exportables if accumulation is undertaken in that country and the reduction in consumption is not confined to engineering products; while Agraria will offer more exportables at constant prices if accumulation is undertaken there and the use of both products for consumption is sought to be reduced.

Thus in this specialization case both the process of accumulation and completed accumulation in Agraria tend to worsen that country's terms of trade, while Mancunia's terms of trade tend to improve as a result of the process of accumulation there and to worsen when the accumulation is completed.

Model Three
Assumptions: Three countries (A, B and C), three products (tools cloth and food), two factors (capital and labour), constant returns to scale in the making of tools and cloth, diminishing returns to scale in agriculture, production of all three products in all three countries, the capital–labour ratio higher in the tools industry than in the cloth industry and lowest in agriculture, no 'inferior' goods in consumption.

We suppose that tools are capital goods alone while food and cloth are used only for consumption purposes.

The products in which each country will have a comparative advantage will be determined by relative cost conditions. We suppose that country A's exportables are tools and cloth and its importable food, that country B's exportable is cloth and its importables tools

79

and food, and that country C's exportable is food and its importables tools and cloth.

Three questions may be considered. First, what is the effect of completed accumulation on the terms of trade of each country, if no further accumulation is undertaken? Secondly, what is the effect of the process of accumulation on the terms of trade of each country? Thirdly, what is the effect of completed accumulation on the terms of trade of each country, if tools continue to be made at a given rate to to be used for further investment?

The answer to the first question is that with only cloth and food being made and a higher capital stock in at least one country, cloth must be cheaper in terms of food. The terms of trade of country A and country B will have deteriorated and those of country C will have improved.

The second question is the effect on the terms of trade of each country of a shift in demand from cloth and food towards tools at constant prices. Tool-making being the most capital-intensive industry, the ratio of capital to labour is reduced in all uses. Wages fall relative to the rate of interest. Cloth will be dearer in terms of food, and tools will be dearer in terms of cloth. Country A's terms of trade will improve, those of country C will worsen and the effect on country B's terms of trade is uncertain.

With regard to the third question, we must conclude that country A's terms of trade will deteriorate and country C's terms of trade will improve, while the effect on country B's terms of trade is uncertain. The reason is that the ratio of capital to labour must be raised in all uses if the output of food or cloth is not to be reduced, and the consequent rise in wages relative to the rate of interest will cheapen products in order of capital intensity.

Model Four

Assumptions: As in Model Three, except that the capital–labour ratio is now assumed to be always higher in the cloth industry than in the tool industry, and higher in the tool industry than in agriculture.

Once more, tools are capital goods and food and cloth are consumer goods.

We continue to assume that relative cost conditions are such that country A's exportables are tools and cloth and its importable food, country B's exportable is cloth and its importables tools and food, and country C's exportable is food and its importables tools and cloth.

As in Model Three, completed accumulation must cheapen cloth in terms of food if no further accumulation is undertaken. The terms of trade of country A and of country B will deteriorate, while those of country C will improve.

We cannot now indicate the directions of change in relative prices as a result of the process of accumulation, irrespective of the relative declines in the demands for food and cloth at constant prices. The making of tools being intermediate in capital intensity, the capital–labour ratio in each industry may either rise or fall as a result of a diversion of demand to tools at constant prices. The greater the fall in cloth consumption relative to food consumption at constant prices in order to buy tools, the more likely it is that the capital–labour ratio in each industry will rise, and vice versa. Let us call a rise in capital–labour ratios case X, and a fall in capital–labour ratios case Y. Under case X, cloth becomes cheaper in terms of tools, and tools fall in price relative to food. The terms of trade of country A and of country B deteriorate, while those of country C improve. Under case Y, cloth is dearer in terms of tools and tools rise in price in terms food. The terms of trade of country A and of country B improve, while those of country C deteriorate.

Completed accumulation will reduce the price of tools in terms of food when tools are produced at a given rate, and the relative price of cloth in terms of tools will also fall. The terms of trade of country A and of country B will deteriorate and those of country C will improve.

The effects on the terms of trade of each country of the process of accumulation and of completed accumulation with tools being produced at a given rate may be summarised as follows, I denoting an improvement, D a deterioration and U an uncertain effect:

	Effect of process of accumulation			Effect of completed accumulation	
	Model Three	Model Four Case X	Model Four Case Y	Model Three	Model Four
Effects on the terms of trade of:					
Country A	I	D	I	D	D
Country B	U	D	I	U	D
Country C	D	I	D	I	I

While in Model One the process of accumulation improved the terms of trade of Mancunia and worsened those of Agraria, we now have the interesting possibility, due to the introduction of a third country and commodity, that the terms of trade of country A (which corresponds to Mancunia) may worsen and those of country C (which corresponds to Agraria) improve both as a result of the process of accumulation and of completed accumulation.

Relatively little can be said regarding the direction of change in country B's terms of trade on the basis of this taxonomic approach, which does not take into account the relative quantities of tools and food imported into that country. On the Model Three assumption that tool-making is more capital intensive than cloth-making, the process of accumulation will tend to worsen country B's terms of trade if it is itself accumulating rapidly and therefore importing mostly tools and little food. On the other hand, completed accumulation abroad will, on these assumptions, be beneficial to country B. If country B is growing slowly, and therefore importing mostly food and few tools, it will benefit from the process of accumulation abroad, but will be worse off when the new equipment comes into use. On the Model Four assumption regarding relative factor intensities, the direction of movement of the terms of trade of country B as a result of the process of accumulation and of completed accumulation is, of course, determinate without reference to the relative importance of tools and food in the country's imports.

Model Five

Assumptions: Three countries (A, B and C), three products (tools, cloth and food), constant or diminishing returns to scale in each industry, specialization by country A in tools, by country B in cloth and by country C in food.

The process of accumulation must improve country A's terms of trade, for more of its product will be demanded at constant prices. The effect on the terms of trade of country B and of country C is uncertain, and will depend on the changes in demand for food and cloth at constant prices.

Completed accumulation must worsen the terms of trade of the country in which accumulation has taken place, if the other two countries have remained stationary. The only exception is when the country whose output has risen wishes to raise its consumption of the commodity in which it specializes by as much or more than the increment in output, at constant prices. For this to happen in country B or country C, the imported consumer good must necessarily be inferior in consumption; while in country A the resources devoted to investment at constant prices must rise by at least the same extent as the increase in output.

REFERENCES

[1] H. G. Johnson, *International Trade and Economic Growth*, London, Allen & Unwin, 1958, Chapter III, pp. 65–93. This is a revised version of the article on 'Economic Expansion and International Trade', *Manchester School of Economic and Social Studies*, Vol. XXIII, 1955, pp. 95–112.

[2] *Ibid.*, Chapter IV, pp. 94–119. This is a reprint of the article on 'Increasing Productivity, Income–Price Trends and the Trade Balance', *Economic Journal*, Vol. LXIV, 1954, pp. 462–85.

8. The Role of Capital-Goods Trade in the Theory of International Trade: Comment[1]

R. E. Baldwin has provided a valuable application of the Fisherian theory of interest to problems of trade and accumulation [1]. He proves that if there are two factors (labour and capital goods) and two products (capital goods and consumption goods), all individuals have identical tastes, the fraction of each individual's income saved varies directly with the interest rate and is invariant with respect to the level of income, and the assumptions, of P. A. Samuelson's interest rate equalization theorem [3] are met, two very interesting propositions hold. First, that, if the *per capita* capital stock is not equal in two countries, product trade cannot remove the incentive to capital movement from the rich to the poor country. This is a conclusion startlingly different from that of Samuelson. Secondly, that product trade will ultimately equalize *per capita* capital stocks between countries, and that trade will then cease.

Baldwin correctly points out that these results hold if an additional capital good is introduced as a produced factor; and that they cease to hold if a natural resource is introduced as an additional factor, even though a second consumption good is introduced so as to ensure that the number of factors does not exceed the number of products.

Baldwin, however, does not appreciate that, if an additional consumption good is introduced in his model, without a natural resource being introduced simultaneously as an additional factor of production, his results equally cease to hold. Suppose that there are two consumption goods (say cloth and food), which are tradeable, and that the capital good is either traded or is produced by each

[1] The author had the benefit of discussion with Paul Samuelson and Jagdish Bhagwati. Baldwin kindly provided helpful comments on earlier drafts.

country to meet its own requirements. We retain all the other assumptions that Baldwin makes. In the current period, trading in cloth and food equalizes product prices, rentals and wages. In Baldwin's model, the expected rental in the next period associated with any given level of investment is that which would prevail if in that period only consumption goods are made. If the factor endowments of countries are sufficiently close, *entrepreneurs* will expect each country to make both cloth and food and to trade in the next period. They will therefore also expect that factor proportions in each industry will be the same in all countries, and that rentals will be equalized.[1]

Once the expected rentals are equalized between countries, so will the expected interest rates, as these interest rates equal the expected rental as a percentage of the current price of a capital good. There will thus be no incentive for international capital movement though *per capita* capital stocks are unequal. The same fraction of income will be saved in all countries. This process will be repeated from period to period until the expected interest rate declines to the level consistent with zero savings. At this stage *per capita* capital stocks need not be equalized. If the fractions of income devoted to cloth and food are the same whatever the level of income, the capital-rich countries will export the more capital-intensive of the two commodities; but if the income-elasticity of demand for the capital-intensive good is high, these countries may export the labour-intensive good.

Baldwin's results thus hinge crucially on the assumption that there is only one consumption good; it is this assumption which entails the conclusions that the expected interest rate must be lower in a capital-rich than in a capital-poor country, and that there is a unique level of the *per capita* capital stock consistent with zero savings.

Therefore Baldwin's model is an inadequate guide to a real world characterized by a multiplicity of consumption goods. It is thus not possible to agree with Baldwin when he concludes that, in view of the declining importance of natural resources as a source of

---

[1] This does not happen in Baldwin's analysis where there is only one consumption good, because when it is expected that this good alone will be produced in each country in the next period it must also be expected that there will be no trade; and with unequal *per capita* capital stocks in different countries, rentals will be expected to vary between countries inversely with the levels of *per capita* capital stocks.

comparative cost differences, *per capita* capital stocks will tend to be equalized between trading countries.

It may be emphasized that in Baldwin's model an incentive is left for funds to move between countries even when factor prices are equalized, because expected rates can diverge and are supposed to govern international flows of funds.[1] In contrast, in Samuelson's model, factor price equalization necessarily leads to interest rate equalization, as the interest rate is the current rental as a percentage of the current price of a capital good.

An important implication of the difference in the interest-theoretic assumptions of Baldwin and Samuelson is that, in Baldwin's model the opening up of trade between a capital-rich and a capital-poor country may actually widen the gap between the rates at which investible funds are traded in these countries. With identical tastes, the pre-trade expected interest rate will be higher in the capital-poor country. Suppose that both countries make both goods when trade is opened up. If investment in each country remains at the pre-trade level, the price of capital goods will rise (fall) in the capital-rich (capital-poor) country. The rentals expected to prevail in each country in the next period do not change when trade is opened up, for entrepreneurs assume that in the next period both countries will make only the consumption good and that there will be no trade. The expected interest rate will therefore fall (rise) in the capital-rich (capital-poor) country. The level of investment may be reduced in the capital-rich country, and this will raise the expected interest rate; the cut in investment cannot, however, be so large as to restore the expected interest rate to the pre-trade level, if future consumption is not an inferior good. In the capital-poor country the level of investment will certainly be higher, as Baldwin points out; and while the expected interest rate may therefore fall below the pre-trade level, a rise in the expected interest rate due to trade being opened up is possible.

Finally, Bladwin's statements that 'trade models that follow the traditional assumption of excluding international movements of capital funds *invariably* (our italics) are set up entirely in static

[1] Baldwin's *actual* interest rate is defined, on the other hand, as the rental in a period as a percentage of the price of a capital good in the previous period. As he points out correctly, factor price equalization will lead to the equilization of this actual interest rate; however, international capital flows are assumed to be governed by differences in expected rather than actual interest rates.

terms,' and that the possibility of net savings and hence of trade in capital goods is ruled out, require amendment. The present author has analysed the effects of accumulation on the terms of trade when trade is balanced, taking trade in capital goods into account. [2].

REFERENCES
1. Baldwin, R. E., 'The Role of Capital Goods Trade in the Theory of International Trade', *American Economic Review*, Vol. 56, September 1965, pp. 841–8.
2. Ramaswami, V. K., 'The Effects of Accumulation on the Terms of Trade', *Economic Journal*, Vol. 70, September 1960, pp. 514–18.
3. Samuelson, P. A., 'Equalization by Trade of the Interest Rate along with the Real Wage', in R. E. Caves, H. G. Johnson and P. B. Kersen (eds.), *Trade, Growth and the Balance of Payments; Essays in honour of Gottfried Haberler*, Chicago, 1965, pp. 35–52.

9. On Two-Sector Neo-Classical Growth[1]

In this paper simple geometric techniques familiar to most economists are used to prove most of the results regarding two-sector neo-classical growth set out in a series of highly mathematical articles in recent years. Additional results are derived for the case in which investment is assumed to be carried to the point at which its marginal efficiency equals the interest rate. The possibility of factor- intensities in the two sectors sometimes being equal is allowed for.[2]

We assume, as in the literature, that:

(1) There are two goods (investment-goods and consumption-goods) and two factors (investment-goods and labour).

(2) The production functions for both goods exhibit constant returns to scale and diminishing returns to varying factor proportions, and are twice-continuously differentiable. In either industry, the ratio of the marginal physical product of investment-goods to the marginal physical product of labour tends to zero (infinity) as the capital-labour ratio tends to infinity (zero); this is the *derivative condition* which plays a crucial role.

(3) Factors are always fully employed and move freely between industries, and the rental (wage) rate equals the marginal value product of investment-goods (labour).

(4.) The labour supply is constant or grows at a constant exogenous rate. Investment-goods depreciate at a fixed rate. It may alternatively be assumed that investment-goods last for ever if the labour force is growing; the sum of the depreciation rate and of the growth rate of the labour force must, however, be positive.

A balanced growth path is one along which the capital stock and

[1] Sukhamoy Chakravarty, M. Datta-Chaudhuri, A. Manne, A. K. Sen and T. N. Srinivasan provided useful comments.

[2] If factor-intensities in the two sectors are always the same and invariably change in the same proportion, we have essentially a one-sector model.

the labour force grow at the same rate (which may be zero), the *per capita* capital stock and the *per capita* output of each good remaining the same for ever. The *per capita* output of investment-goods will be just sufficient to cover depreciation and to equip new entrants to the labour force in the same manner as existing workers. A balanced growth path may be indentified by the level of the *per capita* capital stock which is always maintained along it.

Sufficient conditions for a unique balanced growth path to be reached are that (1) given the level of the *per capita* capital stock the *per capita* gross output of investment-goods is uniquely determined, and (2) the gross output of investment-goods as a fraction of the capital stock decreases monotonically as the *per capita* capital stock rises, tending to zero (infinity) as the *per capita* capital stock tends to infinity (zero).

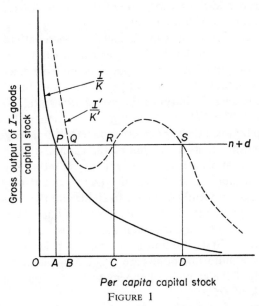

Per capita capital stock

FIGURE 1

In Figure 1, we measure the *per capita* stock of investment-goods along the x-axis and the gross output of investment-goods as a fraction of the capital stock and the sum of the depreciation rate and the growth rate of the labour force along the y-axis. Our first condition ensures that there is a unique level of the gross output of investment-goods as a fraction of the capital stock corresponding to any given level of the *per capita* capital stock; i.e. that short-run equilibrium is unique. Our second condition ensures that the I/K curve depicting the relationship between these variables slopes downward from left to right, approaching the x-(y)axis asymptotically as the *per capita* capital stock tends to infinity (zero). It is easily seen that this curve will cut the horizontal $n + d$ line measuring the sum of the depreciation rate and the growth rate of the labour force at one and only one point; for this line cannot coincide with the x axis, given our assumption that the sum of the depreciation rate and the growth rate of the labour force is positive. Whatever the initial endowment of the economy may be, balanced growth will be reached at P with a *per capita* capital stock of OA; for so long as the *per capita* capital stock is higher (lower) the gross output of investment-goods as a fraction of the capital stock will be lower (higher) than the sum of the depreciation rate and the growth rate of the labour force, and the *per capita* capital stock will fall (rise).

Sufficient conditions for some balanced growth path to be reached are that (1) given the level of the *per capita* capital stock the *per capita* gross output of investment-goods is uniquely determined, and (2) the gross output of investment-goods as a fraction of the capital stock tends to zero (infinity) as the *per capita* capital stock tends to infinity (zero). The I'/K' curve in Figure 1 depicting the one-to-one relationship between the *per capita* capital stock and the gross output of investment-goods as a fraction of the capital stock on these assumptions will approach the x (y-)axis asymptototically as the *per capita* capital stock tends to infinity (zero), but it may not slope downward monotonically from left to right; and there will therefore be at least one point at which it cuts the $n + d$ line. OB, OC and OD are levels of the *per capita* capital stock consistent with balanced growth. If the initial situation is not one of balanced growth, the only possible equilibrium points are Q and S and equilibrium at R is possible only if the economy happens to have initially a *per capita* capital stock of OC.

Three types of assumptions regarding the determination of the level of savings and investment have been made in the literature. First, that the relative quantities demanded of the two goods are constant or depend on their relative prices alone, the expected return from investment-goods having no effect on the demand for them. Income effects are assumed to be absent. This type of assumption is clearly not plausible, but it is of interest to show that these cases can be handled by our method of analysis. Secondly, that a constant fraction of income or constant fractions of the income of each factor are saved. Thirdly, that investment is carried to the point at which its marginal efficiency equals the interest rate. This is the most interesting type of assumption, for it allows for the influence of expected profitability on the level of investment. Savings may be assumed to depend on the income level and the interest rate, or on the level of total income or on the income of each factor.

We discuss short-run equilibrium in Section I and growth paths in Section II. We sum up our results and offer some concluding observations in the final Section. It may be noted that income, outputs, rentals, savings, and investment are throughout defined gross of depreciation.

The assumption that the production of investment-goods is never more capital-intensive than that of consumption-goods is called the *weak* capital-intensity hypothesis, the *strong* capital-intensity hypothesis being that investment-goods are always the more labour-intensive of the two products.

I

We establish in this Section that short-run equilibrium is unique, on various alternative sets of assumptions.

The constant elasticity of substitution in demand between the two goods is not negative. Let us suppose that the relative quantities demanded of the two goods depend on the product-price ratio alone. We first assume that the factor-intensities of the two goods are different. The transformation curve depicting the production frontier with a given endowment must be strictly convex from above, given our assumptions of constant returns to scale and diminishing returns to varying factor proportions. Demand conditions can be represented by indifference curves. If the constant elasticity of substitution is zero, the relative quantities demanded of the two goods being always the same, the indifference curves will be L-shaped, and it is easily seen that short-run equilibrium will be unique at a point at which both goods are made. If the constant elasticity of substitution is positive, the indifference curves will be strictly concave from above, except in the limiting case of infinite elasticity when they will be straight lines. The indifference curves will not cut either axis if the elasticity of substitution is not greater than unity, and both goods will be made in unique short-run equilibrium. When the elasticity of substitution is greater than unity the production of one good alone may be undertaken in unique short-run equilibrium when this good is very cheap at all points on the transformation curve because it is the more (less) capital-intensive good and the *per capita* capital stock is very high (low).

If the factor-intensities of the two goods happen to be the same with the given endowment, the *TT* curve will be a straight line; the characteristics of short-run equilibrium will, however, be the same as in the unequal factor-intensities case. We assume that the transformation and indifference curves are not straight lines with the same slope; in this case short-run equilibrium will of course not be unique.

The constant positive fraction of rentals saved is not less than the constant fraction of wages saved. We first assume that the strong capital-intensity hypothesis is met. Suppose that *A* in Figure 2 is an

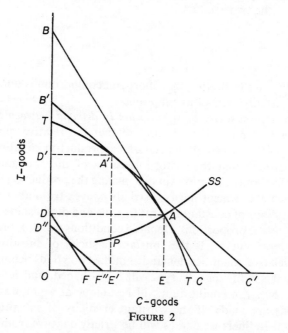

C-goods

FIGURE 2

equilibrium point. Let the tangent to *TT* at *A* be *BAC*, *AD* and *AE* being perpendiculars to the axes from *A*. As income in terms of investment-goods is OB, and savings in terms of these goods are OD, the fraction of income saved is OD/OB. Let A' be any point on TT at which relatively more investment-goods than at A are made, let $B'A'C'$ be the tangent to TT at A', and let $A'D'$ and $A'E'$ be perpendiculars to the axes from A'. Income in terms of investment-goods is OB', which is less than OB. The rental–wage ratio and hence the share of rentals in income is lower, for both industries become more capital-intensive when relatively more of the labour-intensive good is made. The fraction of income saved cannot therefore be higher. Savings in terms of investment-goods cannot exceed the level OD'', at which $OD''/OB' = OD/OB$, and will therefore be lower than the output OD' of these goods.

Income in terms of consumption-goods will no doubt have risen from OC to OC', and savings in terms of these goods will have risen from OF to not more than OF'', where F and F'' are points on the x-axis such that

$$\frac{OD}{OB} = \frac{OF}{OC} \text{ and } \frac{OD''}{OB'} = \frac{OF''}{OC'}$$

However, as the price lines DF and $D''F''$ intersect, the quantity of investment-goods demanded will decline though savings in terms of consumption-goods are larger. The choice of *numéraire* does not affect the results.

Let P be the point on $A'E'$ whose vertical distance $F'P$ ($\leqslant OD''$) from the x-axis measures savings in terms of investment-goods when production is at A'. Then the SS curve, which is the locus of the point P whose vertical distance from the x-axis measures the quantity of investment-goods demanded when the production point coincides with it or lies vertically above or below it will slope upward monotonically from left to right and will cut TT at a single point. In the special case in which the constant fraction of both rentals and wages saved is unity, the SS curve will be the portion of the y-axis not below the point at which the TT curve cuts this axis.

If the factor-intensities in the two industries are the same and the TT curve is a straight line, the SS curve will be a horizontal straight line cutting TT at a single point.

The marginal efficiency of investment equals the interest rate. We now assume that prospective rentals vary inversely with the *per capita* capital stock and the *per capita* output of investment–goods and directly with current rentals, and that investment is carried to the point at which its marginal efficiency equals the interest rate. Given the strong capital-intensity hypothesis, the rental–wage ratio declines when relatively more investment-goods are made. Now for any small change the effect on costs of changes in factor quantities can be ignored; and the current rental on an investment-good as a percentage of its price falls. As prospective rentals vary directly with current rentals and inversely with the output of investment-goods, the marginal efficiency of investment declines.

In Figure 3, the quantity of investment-goods that can be bought

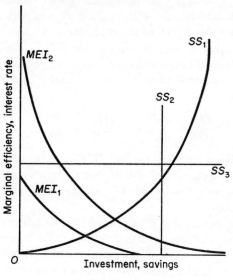

FIGURE 3

from savings and the output of these goods is measured along the x-axis, the length of this axis representing the output of investment-goods when these goods alone are produced. The marginal efficiency of investment and the interest rate are measured along the y-axis. The *MEI* curves depict the relationship between the output of investment-goods and the marginal efficiency of investment. The *SS* curves indicate the interest rate required to induce any given level of savings in terms of investment-goods, or, what comes to the same thing, to induce the saving of a specified fraction of income; for as the relative output of investment-goods rises the fraction of income saved must be larger if savings and investment are to be equal.

The SS_1 curve depicts the case in which the average savings ratio varies directly with the interest rate, tending to unity (zero) as the interest rate tends to infinity (zero). It is easily seen that, given the shape of the SS_1 curve, unique short-run equilibrium exists even if the MEI_1 curve cuts one or both axes.

The MEI_2 curve depicts the case in which the marginal efficiency of investment tends to zero (infinity) as the relative output of investment-goods tends to infinity (zero). If the constant positive fraction of rentals saved is not less than the constant fraction of wages saved, the SS curve is a vertical straight line such as SS_2, and short-run equilibrium is unique. If the interest rate influences savings, but the average savings ratio never increases as the interest rate falls, short-run equilibrium is also unique, for the SS curve will never slope downward from left to right. The SS_3 curve depicts the case in which the supply of savings is perfectly elastic at some positive finite interest rate.

If the average savings ratio never varies inversely with the interest rate or the level of *per capita* income, and the marginal propensity to save does not exceed unity, the SS curve will never slope downward from left to right, and cannot therefore cut the MEI curve at more than one point. The existence of one point of intersection can be ensured without assuming that the marginal efficiency of investment tends to zero (infinity) as the relative output of investment-goods tends to infinity (zero), by stipulating that the average savings ratio never falls below a specified positive level in short-run full-employment equilibrium.

If the factor-intensities of the two goods happen to be the same, the MEI curve will once more slope downward from left to right because prospective rentals decline as more investment-goods are produced. The shape of the SS curve on each assumption regarding the savings function will be the same as in the corresponding unequal factor-intensities case. The conclusions we reached on the assumption that the strong capital-intensity condition is met hold also if only the weak capital-intensity hypothesis is stipulated.

If the production of investment-goods is more capital-intensive than that of consumption-goods, the rental–wage ratio and hence the current rental on an investment-good as a fraction of its price will *rise* as relatively more investment-goods are produced. If prospective rentals equal current rentals the MEI curve will rise monotonically from left to right, and may cut the SS curve at more

95

than one point; multiple short-run equilibria may exist, of which some may be unstable (Figure 4).

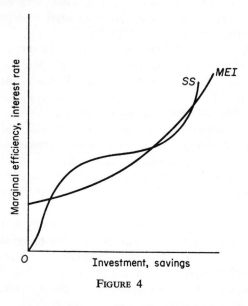

FIGURE 4

II

We now turn to the consideration of growth paths. We first show that the gross output of investment-goods as a fraction of the capital stock tends to zero (infinity) as the *per capita* capital stock tends to infinity (zero), provided that the relative output of consumption-goods does not tend to infinity as the *per capita* capital stock tends to zero. We then prove that, on certain sets of assumptions, the relative output of consumption-goods does not tend to infinity as the *per capita* capital stock tends to zero, and the gross output of investment-goods as a fraction of the capital stock decreases monotonically as the *per capita* capital stock rises; unique balanced growth paths will therefore be reached. Finally we show that, on other sets of assumptions, some balanced growth paths will be reached because the relative output of consumption-goods does not tend to infinity as the *per capita* capital stock tends to zero.

Let us write I for the gross output of investment-goods, C for the output of consumption-goods, K for the capital stock, K_I and K_C for the capital devoted to the production of investment-goods and consumption-goods respectively, and k for the *per capita* capital stock. It is easily seen that

$$\frac{I}{K} = \frac{I}{K_I + K_C}$$

$$= \frac{1}{(K_I/I) + (K_C/C) \cdot (C/I)}$$

Thus the gross output of investment-goods as a fraction of the capital stock is equal to the reciprocal of the sum of (*a*) the reciprocal of the average physical product of capital in the investment-goods industry and (*b*) the product of the reciprocal of the average physical product of capital in the consumption-goods industry and of the relative output of consumption-goods. Now, given the derivative condition, the marginal and hence the average physical product of capital in either industry tends to zero (infinity) as the capital–labour ratio in that industry tends to infinity (zero). Further, as the overall capital–labour ratio tends to infinity (zero) the capital–labour ratios in both industries must tend to infinity (zero); for while the capital–labour ratios in both industries may change for a while in the opposite direction to the overall capital–labour ratio, this entails declining *per capita* output of one of the goods.[1] Demand conditions may rule this out; and even if they do not, a point will be reached at which either one good alone is made—in which case the capital–labour ratio in its production is obviously the overall capital–labour ratio—or both goods are made and capital–labour ratios in both industries move in the same direction as the overall capital–labour ratio.

We can therefore conclude that as the overall capital–labour ratio tends to infinity (zero) the gross output of investment-goods as a fraction of the capital stock tends to zero (infinity), provided that the relative output of consumption-goods does not tend to infinity as the *per capita* capital stock tends to zero; for it is easily seen that given

$$\lim_{k \to 0} \frac{K_I}{I} = 0,$$

$$\lim_{k \to 0} \frac{K_C}{C} = 0,$$

[1] This is proved in [11].

$$\lim_{k \to \infty} \frac{K_I}{I} = \infty,$$

$$\lim_{k \to \infty} \frac{K_C}{C} = \infty,$$

$$\lim_{k \to 0} \frac{C}{I} \neq \infty,$$

we have

$$\lim_{k \to 0} \frac{I}{K} = \lim_{k \to 0} \frac{1}{(K_I/I) + (K_C/C) \cdot (C/I)} = \infty,$$

and

$$\lim_{k \to \infty} \frac{I}{K} = \lim_{k \to 0} \frac{1}{(K_I/I) + (K_C/C) \cdot (C/I)} = 0$$

It may be noted that we do not need to make any assumption regarding the limit to which the relative output of consumption-goods tends as the *per capita* capital stock tends to infinity.

We now consider unique balanced growth paths.

The constant elasticity of substitution in demand is zero. The transformation curves in Figure 5 are normalized on a *per capita* basis,

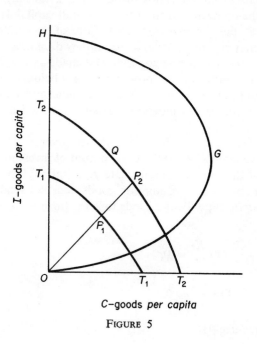

C–goods *per capita*

FIGURE 5

the *per capita* capital stock being higher when the transformation curve is T_2T_2 than when it is T_1T_1. When the constant elasticity of substitution in demand is zero the relative quantities demanded of the two goods are always the same, and OP_1P_2 is the radiant from the origin on which all equilibrium points lie. With production at P_2 instead of P_1 both industries are more capital-intensive and the equal proportionate increase in the *per capita* output of both goods will be less than the proportionate increase in the *per capita* capital stock. The gross output of investment-goods as a fraction of the capital stock will therefore be lower; and we can conclude that it falls monotonically as the *per capita* capital stock rises. As the relative output of consumption-goods is constant, it does not tend to infinity as the *per capita* capital stock tends to zero; and a unique balanced growth path will be reached. No assumption regarding the relative factor-intensities of the two goods is necessary.

The constant elasticity of substitution in demand is positive. We assume initially that the strong capital-intensity hypothesis is met. Let P_1 be the equilibrium point when the transformation curve is T_1T_1. Consumption-goods will be relatively cheaper with production at P_2, for they are the more capital-intensive good and both industries are more capital-intensive. As the constant elasticity of substitution in demand is positive relatively more consumption-goods than at P_2 will be produced when the transformation curve is T_2T_2. But the gross output of investment-goods as a fraction of the capital stock declines even when the production point shifts from P_1 to P_2; and we can conclude that it falls monotonically as the *per capita* capital stock rises. As the relative output of consumption-goods declines as the *per capita* capital stock falls, it does not tend to infinity as the *per capita* capital stock tends to zero; and a unique balanced growth path will be reached.

The above analysis holds also if only the weak capital-intensity hypothesis is met and T_2T_2 is a straight line. Now suppose that T_1T_1 is a straight line. When the *per capita* capital stock is slightly higher the product-price ratio remains the same, as the effects on costs of changes in factor-proportions can be ignored for any small change; the relative quantities produced of the two goods will therefore be the same, and once more we can conclude that a unique balanced growth path will be reached.

The constant positive fraction of rentals saved is not less than the constant fraction of wages saved. We first assume that the strong capital-intensity hypothesis is met. We use investment-goods as the *numéraire*, for the sake of simplicity; our proof holds also if instead consumption-goods are the *numéraire*.

Let Q be a point on T_2T_2 at which the proportionate rise in *per capita* output of investment-goods, relative to production at the initial equilibrium point P_1, is equal to the proportionate increase in the *per capita* capital stock. The relative output and the relative price of investment-goods will be higher with production at Q than with production at P_2 and hence than with production at P_1.

When the production point shifts from P_1 to P_2 the proportionate rise in *per capita* income is less than the equal proportionate increase in *per capita* output of both goods and hence less than the proportionate rise in the *per capita* capital stock. With production at Q income is less than with production at P_2, and hence we conclude that when the production points shifts from P_1 to Q the proportionate rise in *per capita* income will be less than the proportionate rise in the *per capita* capital stock.

Suppose that when the production point shifts from P_1 to Q the rental rate remains unchanged. Then rentals and savings from rentals *per capita* will rise in the same proportion as the *per capita* capital stock. The proportionate rise in wages and hence in savings from wages *per capita* must, however, be less than the proportionate increase in the *per capita* capital stock, for we have seen that income *per capita* will have risen proportionately less than the *per capita* capital stock. Savings *per capita* will therefore have increased proportionately less than the *per capita* capital stock and the *per capita* output of investment-goods; and relatively less investment-goods than at Q will be produced when the transformation curve is T_2T_2.

It may be noted that the rental rate must in fact be lower with production at Q than with production at P_1; what our argument shows is that the gross output of investment-goods as a fraction of the capital stock declines when the *per capita* capital stock rises, even if the fall in the rental–wage ratio when both industries are more capital-intensive is very small.

The relative output of consumption-goods will not tend to infinity as the *per capita* capital stock tends to zero, for as the *per capita* capital stock declines the rental–wage ratio and the relative price of consumption-goods increase; and we can conclude that a unique balanced growth path will be reached.

If it is assumed that the weak capital-intensity hypothesis is fulfilled and the T_2T_2 is a straight line while T_1T_1 is convex from above, the relative output and the relative price of the two goods and the rental–wage ratio will be the same at Q and P_2. It is easily seen that the conclusion that when the production point shifts from P_1 to Q the proportionate rise in savings in terms of investment-goods will be less than the proportionate increase in the output of these goods still holds.

If T_1T_1 is a straight line, and there is a small rise in the *per capita* capital stock, the product–price ratio will not change, but the rental–wage ratio will be lower. If the output of investment-goods is such that the *per capita* capital stock is maintained intact, *per capita* income in terms of these goods will rise proportionately less than the *per capita* capital stock, and with a lower rental–wage ratio savings in terms of investment-goods will be less than the output of these goods. We can conclude that the weak capital-intensity hypothesis is a sufficient condition for a unique balanced growth path to be reached.

The average savings ratio varies directly with the interest rate, or the marginal efficiency is always positive and finite. We now assume that the strong or the weak capital-intensity hypothesis is met, and that (*a*) the average savings ratio varies directly with the interest rate, tending to unity (zero) as the interest rate tends to infinity (zero), or (*b*) the marginal efficiency of investment with any given endowment varies inversely with the relative output of investment-goods, tending to zero (infinity) as the relative output of investment-goods tends to infinity (zero), and (1) the average savings ratio never rises as the interest rate falls, or (2) the constant positive fraction of rentals saved is not less than the constant fraction of wages saved.

Suppose that P_1 is the initial equilibrium point. With production at P_2 the marginal efficiency of investment will be lower than with production at P_1, for the *per capita* capital stock and the *per capita* output of investment-goods are higher and current rentals are lower. The fraction of income required to be saved is, however, higher or the same; and if the interest rate influences savings and the average savings ratio never rises as the interest rate decreases, the interest rate that equates savings in terms of investment-goods with the output of these goods will be higher than the marginal efficiency of investment with production at P_2. Relatively less investment-goods than at P_2 will be produced when the transformation curve is T_2T_2;

101

and we can conclude that the gross output of investment-goods as a fraction of the capital stock falls monotonically as the *per capita* capital stock rises. The relative output of consumption-goods does not tend to infinity as the *per capita* capital stock tends to zero, for it declines as the *per capita* stock decreases. Unique balanced growth will thus be reached.

We have already seen that if the level of investment is not influenced by the interest rate, and the constant positive fraction of rentals saved is not less than the constant fraction of wages saved, unique balanced growth will be attained. This analysis holds fully if it assumed that (*a*) the marginal efficiency of investment with any given endowment varies inversely with the relative output of investment-goods, tending to zero (infinity) as the relative output of investment-goods tends to infinity (zero), and (*b*) the constant positive fraction of rentals saved is not less than the constant positive fraction of wages saved. What the assumption regarding the marginal efficiency schedule does is to ensure that *entrepreneurs* will borrow and invest at some positive finite interest rate the fixed level of savings forthcoming under full employment with any given endowment.

We now turn to the consideration of non-unique balanced growth paths.

The constant elasticity of substitution in demand is positive and not greater than unity. We do not make any assumption regarding the relative factor-intensities of the two goods. We assume that the constant elasticity of substitution in demand between the two goods is positive and not greater than unity. A special case is that of unit elasticity, with a constant fraction of income being saved. The relative output of consumption-goods cannot tend to infinity as the *per capita* capital stock tends to zero, even if these are the less capital-intensive goods; for the fraction of income devoted to them cannot rise as the *per capita* capital stock declines. Some balanced growth path will therefore be reached.

The average savings ratio has a positive floor. Suppose that the weak capital-intensity hypothesis is met, the average savings ratio never varies inversely with the interest rate or the level of *per capita* income, the marginal propensity to save does not exceed unity, and short-run full-employment equilibrium with the average savings ratio not below a specified positive level always exists. The assumption that the average savings ratio never falls below a specified positive level is sufficient to ensure that the relative output of consumption-goods does not tend to infinity as the *per capita* capital stock tends to zero; and we can conclude that some balanced growth path will be reached.

III

We have proved that a unique balanced growth path will be reached if one of the following sets of conditions is met:

(1) The elasticity of substitution in demand between the two goods is always zero. No assumption regarding the relative factor-intensities of the two goods is necessary.[1]

(2) The weak capital-intensity hypothesis is stipulated, and (a) the elasticity of substitution in demand between the two goods is constant and positive,[2] (b) the constant positive fraction of rentals saved is not less than the constant fraction of wages saved.[3] The assumption that a constant fraction of income is saved is a special case both of (a) (as it is equivalent to the assumption of constant unit elasticity of substitution in demand) and of (b).[4]

(3) When the expected return on investment influences its level, the weak capital-intensity hypothesis ensures that the marginal efficiency of investment schedule is 'well-ordered' in the sense that the marginal efficiency varies inversely with the *per capita* capital stock and the *per capita* output of investment-goods, if prospective rentals vary directly with current rentals and inversely with the *per capita* capital stock and the *per capita* output of investment-goods. Given the weak capital-intensity hypothesis, the further alternative sets of assumptions that are sufficient for a unique balanced growth path to be reached are that: (a) the average savings ratio increases monotonically as the interest rate rises,[5] tending to unity (zero) as the interest rate tends to infinity (zero), or (b) the marginal efficiency of investment decreases monotonically as the level of investment rises with a given capital stock, tending to zero (infinity) as the

---

[1] We have extended Inada's result [6] that when the constant elasticity of substitution is not negative *and the strong capital-intensity hypothesis is met* a unique balanced growth path will be reached, in so far as the case of zero elasticity is concerned.

[2] This is proved in [6] with the strong capital-intensity hypothesis.

[3] This is proved in [2] with the strong capital-intensity hypothesis.

[4] This case is discussed in [14] with the strong capital-intensity hypothesis.

[5] This implies that at any given interest rate the marginal propensity to save equals the average propensity to save.

relative output of investment-goods tends to infinity (zero); and (i) the interest rate influences savings and the average savings ratio never rises as the interest rate falls, or (ii) savings are not dependent on the interest rate and a constant positive fraction of income is saved or the constant positive fraction of rentals saved is not less than the constant fraction of wages saved.[1]

We have also shown that some balanced growth path will be reached if one of the following sets of conditions is met:

(1) The elasticity of substitution in demand between the two goods is positive and not greater than unity. No assumption regarding the relative factor-intensities of the two goods is necessary.[2]

(2) The expected profitability of investment influences its level, the weak capital-intensity hypothesis is met, the average savings ratio never varies inversely with the interest rate or the level of *per capita* income, the marginal propensity to save does not exceed unity, and the marginal efficiency and savings schedules are such that with any given endowment some full-employment equilibrium exists at which the average savings ratio is not below a specified positive level.[3]

It is of interest to consider the relationship between the alternative assumptions that we have made on the demand side. Constant unit elasticity of substitution in demand is mathematically equivalent to a constant fraction of income being saved. In short-run analysis, constant elasticity of substitution of more (less) than unity entails that the fraction of income saved varies directly (inversely) with income, for the following reason. As relatively fewer investment-goods are made with a given endowment, they become relatively cheaper, and the fraction of income devoted to their purchase rises (falls) if the constant elasticity of substitution is greater (less) than unity. Income in terms of these goods rises. So the assumption of a constant elasticity of substitution of less than unity contradicts the generally accepted view that the marginal propensity to save varies directly with income.

When the *per capita* capital stock rises, and the strong capital-

[1] These cases have not been discussed in the literature. We have not considered the model in [7], as in this model short-run equilibrium may be at a negative interest rate.

[2] This is proved in [6].

[3] This is proved in [14] with the strong capital-intensity hypothesis.

intensity hypothesis holds, the fraction of income devoted to investment-goods rises (falls) if the constant elasticity of substitution is less (greater) than unity. If *per capita* income in terms of these goods rises, a constant elasticity of substitution of more than unity entails that the marginal propensity to save varies inversely with income. So even if there is no perverse relationship between income and savings in the short run, because the constant elasticity of substitution is greater than unity, the fraction of income saved may decline as the *per capita* capital stock and *per capita* income rise.

If investment-goods are more capital-intensive than consumption-goods, and the constant elasticity of substitution is less than unity, the fraction of income devoted to investment-goods falls as the *per capita* capital stock rises. If *per capita* income in terms of investment-goods increases, we have a perverse long-run relationship between income and savings. We have shown that some balanced growth path will be reached, irrespective of the relative capital-intensities of the two goods, if the constant elasticity of substitution is positive and less than unity; but this result is based on an invariably perverse short-run and possibly perverse long-run relationship between income and savings.

Thus our conclusions regarding balanced growth paths being reached on the assumption of a constant elasticity of substitution other than unity must be regarded as unrealistic. It is in any case implausible to assume that the relative demand for the two goods depends only on their relative prices, and not at all on income or the expected return on investment.

It should be noted that the marginal efficiency of investment schedule specified in models of this kind is qualitatively different from that of Keynes. Shifts of the schedule due to changed expectations must be ruled out in neo-classical growth models; the relationship between the *per capita* capital stock, the *per capita* output of investment-goods, and the expected rate of return remains unchanged for all time. Note also that the form of the savings function or the marginal efficiency of investment schedule is assumed to be such that full employment equilibrium always exists; here too we have a basic departure from the Keynesian model.

In a well-known paper, Lerner said that the social marginal efficiency of investment will be less than, equal to, or greater than the social marginal productivity of capital depending on whether net investment is positive, zero, or negative; he implicitly assumed a constant labour force [8]. He later thought that the question whether the interest rate is equal to the marginal product of capital in long-run stationary equilibrium is essentially meaningless, because no problem about capital but only problems about investment can ever arise [9]. It is nevertheless of interest to note that in our two-good model the marginal product of capital can be defined as the marginal efficiency of investment when the relative output of investment-goods is just sufficient to keep the *per capita* capital stock unchanged, and expected rentals equal current rentals.

The *OGH* curve in Figure 5 is the locus of the short-run equilibrium point with a given endowment at which the economy will be in a steady state. As the *per capita* capital stock increases the relative output of investment-goods consistent with a steady state will rise, for the equal proportionate rise in the *per capita* output of both goods that is feasible will be less than the proportionate increase in the *per capita* capital stock. The *per capita* output of consumption-goods will rise up to the Golden Rule point (*G* in Figure 5) and decline thereafter.

As has been shown in [1], the marginal product of capital will decline monotonically as the *per capita* capital stock rises, irrespective of the relative factor-intensities of the two goods and of whether the *per capita* capital stock is below or above the Golden Rule level. To prove this simply, we use our identity

$$\frac{I}{K} = \frac{1}{(K_I/I) - (K_C/C) \cdot (C/I)}$$

I/K has the same value in all Golden Ages, being equal to the sum of the growth rate of the labour force and the depreciation rate. C/I will be lower in a Golden Age with a larger *per capita* capital stock, for I/K cannot be held constant unless the relative output of investment-goods increases. The average physical product of capital in both industries and hence the marginal product of capital must be lower.[1]

---

[1] Capital–labour ratios in the two industries cannot move in opposite directions. We may think of the move from one Golden Age to another with more capital *per* head as consisting of two steps. In step 1 the relative quantities made of the two goods when the *per capita* capital stock is larger is such that techniques are unchanged. Step 2 is a movement along the new transformation curve to the Golden Age production point; and this clearly cannot change factor proportions in the two industries in opposite directions.

The capital-intensity hypothesis has generally been regarded as not having any particular economic significance, and surprise has often been expressed that so much should depend on what Solow has described as 'a casual property of the technology' [12]. It would appear that in fact the weak capital-intensity hypothesis is the condition that technology must satisfy if it is not to exhibit increasing returns in the sense that the relative cost of future consumption in terms of current consumption foregone falls as relatively more current consumption is given up in order to provide for the future.

REFERENCES

1. Burmeister, E., 'The Existence of Golden Ages and Stability in the Two-Sector Model', *Quarterly Journal of Economics*, Vol. LXXXI, No. 1, February 1967, pp. 146–54.
2. Drandakis, E. M., 'Factor-substitution in the Two-Sector Model', *Review of Economic Studies*, Vol. XXX (3), No. 84, October, 1963, pp. 217–28.
3. Hahn, F. H., 'On Two-Sector Growth Models', *Review of Economic Studies*, Vol. XXXII (4), No. 92, October 1965, pp. 339–46.
4. Hahn, F. H. and Matthews, R. C. O., 'The Theory of Economic Growth: A Survey', *Economic Journal*, Vol. LXXIV, No. 296, December 1964, pp. 770–902.
5. Inada, K., 'On a Two-Sector Model of Economic Growth: Comments and a Generalization', *Review of Economic Studies*, Vol. XXX (2), No. 83, June 1963, pp. 119–27.
6. Inada, K., 'On the Stability of Growth Equilibria in Two-Sector Models', *Review of Economic Studies*, Vol. XXXI (2), No. 86, April 1964, pp. 127–42.
7. Inada, K., 'On Neo-Classical Models of Economic Growth', *Review of Economic Studies*, Vol. XXXII (2), No. 90, April 1965, pp. 151–60.
8. Lerner, A. P., 'Capital, Investment and Interest', *Essays in Economic Analysis*, London, 1953, pp. 347–53.
9. Lerner, A. P., 'On the Marginal Product of Capital and the Marginal Efficiency of Investment', *Journal of Political Economy*, Vol. LXI (1), February 1953, pp. 1–14.
10. Meade, J. E., *A Neo-Classical Theory of Economic Growth*, London, Allen & Unwin, 1961.
11. Rybczynski, T. M., 'Factor Endowment and Relative Commodity Prices', *Economica*, NS Vol. XXII, No. 88, November 1955, pp. 336–41.
12. Solow, R. M., 'Note on Uzawa's Two-Sector Model of Economic Growth', *Review of Economic Studies*, Vol. XXIX (1), No. 78, October 1961, pp. 48–50.
13. Uzawa, H., 'On a Two-Sector Model of Economic Growth', *Review of Economic Studies*, Vol. XXIX (1), No. 78, October 1961, pp. 40–7.
14. Uzawa, H., 'On a Two-Sector Model of Economic Growth: II', *Review of Economic Studies*, Vol. XXX (2), No. 83, June 1963, pp. 105–18.

10. International Factor Movement and the National Advantage[1]

Suppose that a capital-rich country, Mancunia, and a capital-poor country, Agraria, each use capital (K) and labour (L) to make the same good, the common production function $\phi = F(K, L)$ exhibiting constant returns to scale and diminishing returns to varying factor proportions. Initially there is no factor movement because of Mancunian prohibitions. Mancunia now wishes to secure the factor movement which maximizes its *per capita* income, and is sure that Agraria will not retaliate. The policy measure considered in the literature[2] is the optimal restriction of investment in Agraria, the implicit assumption being made that labour is immobile. Using subscripts m and a to denote countries, foreign investment I is optimal when

$$\frac{\partial F}{\partial K_m} = \frac{\partial F}{\partial K_a} + \frac{\partial^2 F}{\partial K_a^2}$$

A tax on earnings of capital invested abroad or direct controls can be employed indifferently to secure the optimal level of foreign investment; when a tax is used, the optimal rate is

$$\left(\frac{\partial F}{\partial K_a} - \frac{\partial F}{\partial K_m}\right) \bigg/ \left(\frac{\partial F}{\partial K_a}\right) = \left(-I\frac{\partial^2 F}{\partial K_a^2}\right) \bigg/ \left(\frac{\partial F}{\partial K_a}\right)$$

The *per capita* income of Mancunian natives will be higher, however, if an optimal tax is levied on immigrant earnings and foreign investment is prohibited. Suppose that Mancunia, having invested optimally abroad, withdraws its capital and permits immigration of the workers using Mancunian capital in Agraria. As the *per capita* capital stock in Agraria is unchanged, immigrants need only be paid the wage they received hitherto; and if they continued to work with

---

[1] P. Bardhan provided useful comments.

[2] One-good models are analysed in [2], [3] and [5]. The assumption that capital alone is mobile is also made in recent analysis of a two-goods model [1], [4].

the same amount of capital per head as was previously employed in Agraria, Mancunian natives are no better or no worse off. But Mancunian natives can become better off by adopting a *uniform* capital–labour ratio for all production in Mancunia, taxing the earnings of immigrants so as to keep their net wages constant and distributing the tax proceeds among natives. Thus *some* tax rate on immigrant earnings exists which secures higher *per capita* income for Mancunian natives than would the optimal restriction of foreign investment. The optimal labour inflow is such that

$$\frac{\partial F}{\partial L_m} = \frac{\partial F}{\partial L_a} - \frac{\partial^2 F}{\partial L_a^2}$$

where M denotes the volume of immigration; and the optimal tax rate on immigrants' earnings is

$$\left(\frac{\partial F}{\partial L_m} - \frac{\partial F}{\partial L_a}\right) \Big/ \left(\frac{\partial F}{\partial L_m}\right) = \left(-M\frac{\partial^2 F}{\partial L_a^2}\right) \Big/ \left(\frac{\partial F}{\partial L_m}\right)$$

Quantitative restriction of immigration obviously is inferior to the levy of an optimal tax on immigrants' earnings. It is in fact inferior even to a policy of permitting free factor movement: if immigrants must be paid the same net wage as domestic labour, immigration contributes to the income of natives until the point is reached at which the marginal products of labour in the two countries are equalized.

If it is Agraria that wishes to induce the factor movements which will maximize the *per capita* income of its natives, *including emigrants,* the first-best policy is to tax optimally the earnings of imported capital, and the second-best policy is to restrict emigration optimally. If, however, the *per capita* income of natives who continue to reside in Agraria is to be maximized, the optimal policy is to permit free factor movement.

We have shown that when national income, inclusive of income earned abroad by factors of domestic origin, is to be maximized, optimal taxation of the import of the scarce factor is preferable to optimal restriction of the export of the abundant factor. The reason for this asymmetry is as follows. In either case, the optimal restriction ensures equality of the foreign marginal cost (return) from the country's point of view with domestic return (cost). When a country exports its abundant factor, however, it uses that factor more intensively abroad than at home; and import of the scarce factor eliminates the loss on this account.

REFERENCES

[1] Jones, R. W., 'International Capital Movements and the Theory of Tariffs and Trade', *Quarterly Journal of Economics*, Vol. LXXXI, 1967, pp. 1–38.

[2] Kemp, M. C. 'The Benefits and Costs of Private Investment from Abroad: Comment', *Economic Record*, Vol. 38, 1962, pp. 108–9.

[3] ——————, 'Foreign Investment and National Advantage' *Economic Record*, Vol. 38, 1962, pp 56–62,

[4] ——————, 'The Gain from International Trade and Investment: A Neo-Heckscher-Ohlin Approach', *American Economic Review*, Vol. LVI, 1966, pp. 788–809.

[5] MacDougall, G. D. A. 'The Benefits and Costs of Private Investment from Abroad: A Theoretical Approach', *Economic Record*, Vol. 36, 1960, pp. 13–35.

11. Reply

The central point made by L. R. Webb [2] in his valuable Comment on [1] is that, if Mancunia can do an all-or-nothing deal under which it appropriates virtually all the increase in Agraria's income, then the first-best policy for the exercise of Mancunia's national monopoly power entails the maximization of world income. This is of course entirely true. In these circumstances Mancunia maximizes the difference between world income and Agraria's initial income; and as the latter term is a constant, world income must be maximized.

Webb discusses the case in which factors always belong to the country of origin. An all-or-nothing deal is in fact also the first-best policy for Agraria when that country seeks to maximize the *per capita* income of natives who continue to reside in that country (hereafter called 'residents'). The conventional monopoly solution, which will in this case also maximize world income, is that Agraria should prohibit capital movement and allow free emigration of labour. *Per capita* income of Agrarian residents will then equal output *per* resident.[1] The first-best policy for Agraria is to make the freeing of emigration conditional on the surrender by Mancunian natives of virtually all the increase in their incomes as a result of labour inflow from Agraria.[2]

The strategy suggested by Webb is applicable to other fields also. Consider for example the opening up of product trade between Mancunia and Agraria, with factors continuing to be internationally

---

[1] I had said erroneously in my paper that Agraria should permit free factor movement (*op. cit.*, p. 310). This policy may result in some Mancunian capital being invested in Agraria. If this happens, the *per capita* income of Agrarian residents will equal output *minus* earnings of foreign capital, divided by the number of residents. This is clearly lower than output *per* resident.

[2] If Mancunia regards the increase in income of prospective immigrants when they move from Agraria as a benefit, this amount also can be appropriated by Agraria under the all-or-nothing deal. But it is implausible to assume that Mancunia will attach weight to the welfare of prospective immigrants.

111

immobile.[1] Free trade maximizes world income. So Mancunia's first-best policy for the exercise of national monopoly power is to maintain free trade on the basis of an all-or-nothing deal under which it appropriates virtually all of Agraria's gains from trade. When such an all-or-nothing deal is feasible, the levy of an optimum tariff is a second-best policy.

REFERENCES

[1] Ramaswami, V. K., 'International Factor Movement and National Advantage', *Economica*, Vol. XXXV, 1968, pp. 309–10. This constitutes chapter 10 of the present volume.
[2] Webb, L. R. 'International Factor Movement and National Advantage: Comment', *Economica* Vol. XXXVII, 1930, pp. 81–4;

---

[1] We now assume that there are two or more goods and that product price ratios differ in the two countries before trade is opened up.

12. Trade Imbalance, Gains from Trade and National Income Change

This paper examines the implications of foreign trade imbalance for: (i) measurement of the gains from trade; (ii) comparisons of real national income at different periods; and (iii) the multiplier analysis.

I. TRADE IMBALANCE AND THE GAINS FROM TRADE

The Classical economists were interested in obtaining a measure of variations in the gains from foreign trade. While the theory of comparative costs was used to explain the reason for trade, the terms of trade were regarded, with qualifications, as a measure of the gains from trade. This was the purpose for which J. S. Mill and Ricardo used the terms-of-trade concept[11]. Marshall applied the concept of consumers' surpluses to the gains from trade. Consumers' surpluses could not, however, be measured, and Taussig and Haberler discussed the use of terms-of-trade-indices as indicating changes in the gains trade. In later discussion, however, specific consideration has not been given to the use of the terms of trade as a measure of the gains from trade. The recent analysis has been in terms of opportunity costs and demand indifference curves[10]. While such analysis reveals the possibility of improvement through the use of tariffs in the absence of retaliation, it provides no measure of an improvement or deterioration in the conditions of interchange. In applied economic analysis the assumption continues to be made that the changes in the terms of trade are of relevance from the gains from trade stand-point. It is necessary to re-examine the basis for the assumption.

The terms of trade are considered to be significant from the welfare stand-point because they measure changes in the amount of imports a unit of exports can buy. Other things being equal, an improvement in the terms of trade would be assumed to imply an increase in welfare because more imports can be had than before without any change in exports. It is recognized that variations in the composition of trade create ambiguities. There is, however, another important type of ambiguity created by the existence of trade imbalance.

This is seen if the method of construction of terms-of-trade indices is examined. The indices are usually of the price or barter type. The price terms of trade are derived by calculating the relative changes in export and import prices, and the barter terms of trade by calculating the relative changes in quantities of imports and exports. In both cases, only commodity trade or, at any rate, flows of goods and services are taken into account. The composition of trade assumed may vary, but generally either the base-year weighting (Laspeyres-type index) or the current-year weighting (Paasche-type index) is taken for all indices. It is useful, in the first instance, to write down the terms-of-trade indices of both Laspeyres and Paasche types.

Let us write:

p_0, price of imports in base year;

q_0, quantity of imports in base year;

p_1, price of imports in later year;

q_1, quantity of imports in later year;

p_0', price of exports in base year;

q_0', quantity of exports in base year;

p_1', price of exports in later year;

q_1', quantity of exports in later year.

Then the Laspeyres and Paasche price and barter terms-of-trade indices may be written as follows, on the convention that a rise denotes an improvement:

Laspeyres price terms-of-trade index—

$$\frac{\Sigma p_1' q_0'}{\Sigma p_0' q_0'} \div \frac{\Sigma p_1 q_0}{\Sigma p_0 q_0} = \frac{\Sigma p_1' q_0'}{\Sigma p_1 q_0} \times \frac{\Sigma p_0 q_0}{\Sigma p_0' q_0'} \quad \dots\dots\dots(1)$$

Paasche price terms-of-trade index—

$$\frac{\Sigma p_1' q_1'}{\Sigma p_0' q_1'} \div \frac{\Sigma p_1 q_1}{\Sigma p_0 q_1} = \frac{\Sigma p_0 q_1}{\Sigma p_0' q_1'} \times \frac{\Sigma p_1' q_1'}{\Sigma p_1 q_1} \quad \dots\dots\dots\dots(2)$$

Laspeyres barter terms-of-trade index—

$$\frac{\Sigma p_0 q_1}{\Sigma p_0 q_0} \div \frac{\Sigma p_0' q_1'}{\Sigma p_0' q_0'} = \frac{\Sigma p_0 q_1}{\Sigma p_0' q_1'} \times \frac{\Sigma p_0' q_0'}{\Sigma p_0 q_0} \quad \dots\dots\dots(3)$$

Paasche barter terms-of-trade index—

$$\frac{\Sigma p_1 q_1}{\Sigma p_1 q_0} \div \frac{\Sigma p_1' q_1'}{\Sigma p_1' q_0'} = \frac{\Sigma p_1' q_0'}{\Sigma p_1 q_0} \times \frac{\Sigma p_1 q_1}{\Sigma p_1' q_1'} \quad \dots\dots\dots(4)$$

We will, for the present, ignore the composition factor. If there is trade balance in both the years or the degree of trade imbalance is identical, the price and barter terms of trade have the same value. If however, the degree of trade imbalance changes between the two years, the price and barter terms of trade give different results. The ratio of the price terms of trade index to the barter terms of trade index in the current year will be equal to the ratio of the value of imports to the value of exports in the base year divided by the ratio of the value of imports to the value of exports in the current year. It becomes necessary to inquire into the significance of each of these indices.

Taussig([1], p.162) considered this problem in relation to reparation payments. He suggested that when an export surplus was necessary in the current year in order to finance reparation payments, the barter terms-of-trade index was a more suitable measure than the price terms-of-trade index. His argument was that exports used to pay reparations were a loss to the economy and that the price terms-of-trade index assumed that such exports were also available to buy imports. Haberler([1], pp.162-165) has criticized this argument by pointing out that its application is too narrow. He suggested that in each case of imbalance, it was necessary to consider the reasons for the imbalance. It cannot be assumed that all exports which do not buy imports in a given year are a loss to the economy. Haberler did not, however, go on to consider the manner in which the terms of trade could be generally applied to measure the gains from trade.

The fact of the matter is that the price terms of trade and the barter terms of trade are each constructed on an extreme assumption. The price terms-of-trade index assumes that full advantage is taken of the rates of interchange possible due to introduction of money as a commodity, but that money is not actually used in settlement. Exports are assumed to be converted into money and the entire proceeds used to buy imports. The barter terms-of-trade index is calculated on the assumption that exchange is only between goods; while prices affect the weights, a balance of trade after exploiting the possibility of interchange through money is not assumed. Exports in a period are assumed to exchange completely for imports in the period. Neither of the indices represents the terms of interchange on the basis of full settlement when there is trade imbalance. Thus, suppose that in the base year there is balance of trade and in the current year an export surplus. The price terms of trade will be higher than the barter terms of trade in the current year. This situation is, however, possible because in the current year gold is being imported or credits are being given. If it were necessary to ensure a balance in the current year, the initial reaction would be a deterioration in the price terms of trade and an improvement in the barter terms of trade. Whatever the final result, it is unlikely that the price and barter terms of trade will be at the same level with a balance as with trade imbalance. The fact of money import or export permits of a variation in the rate of interchange.

A measure based on partial exchange cannot have significance as measuring the gains from trade. If the terms of trade are to provide a measure of the gains from trade, it is necessary to adjust the method of calculation so as to provide for complete interchange. This can be done only by including money flows specifically in the compilation of terms-of-trade indices. Once this is done, the terms of trade could be used as a measure of the gains from trade on the basis of the Hicks–Scitovsky criteria for an improvement[3,8].

The introduction of money flows into the construction of terms-of-trade indices in this manner brings us back to the composition problem. This can be solved in the usual way by saying that the indices with each composition set limits to the 'true' value. The new commodity problem in comparing a year of balance and a year of imbalance is not serious. This can be got over by expressing money in an extremely small quantitative unit. Then, for practical purposes, the value of money taken in the year of balance will be negligible. The increased amount in the other year would, of course, be expressed as an increased quantity, the price remaining the same.

II. TRADE IMBALANCE AND COMPARISONS OF REAL NATIONAL INCOME

The existence of foreign trade, and in particular the possibility of trade imbalance, has relevance to the discussion regarding comparison of real national income at different periods. The distinction has been drawn in the national-income discussion between measures of consumer welfare and measures of productivity or production potential[3,4,6,7]. It is necessary to examine how foreign trade can be fitted into these measures.

Regarding the measure of consumer welfare, the possibility of trade imbalance suggests that private savings should be treated as postponenment of purchase of consumption goods rather than as purchase of investment goods. This corresponds to Professor Hicks' view in his original article[3] and to Mr Little's[7] view. The alternative course suggested by Professor Kuznets[6] has the disadvantage that a part of savings may finance an export surplus or that a part of investment may be financed by an import surplus. If investment goods rather than savings are to be counted, specific account would also have to be taken of gold inflows and outflows. In regard to the foreign-imbalance part, at any rate, the assumption would have to be made that the motive for saving or dissaving is the desire to postpone or accelerate consumption. It would be more consistent to treat all savings as equivalent to postponement of purchase of consumption goods.

In regard to the measure of production potential, the introduction of foreign trade creates serious difficulties. The relationship between production goods and consumption goods would be affected by variations in the terms of trade. This is so even if only consumption goods enter into foreign trade. Exported consumption goods would have to be regarded as producer goods which secure the imported consumption goods. The assumption would have to be made that the relation between marginal costs and prices is uniform not only within the economy but also in other economies in relation to goods entering into foreign trade. This is clearly a more difficult assumption to make.

When there is trade imbalance, the production potential measure needs to take account of the flows of money. International currency is in this context a producer good enabling acquisition of consumer goods in the future on more favourable terms as a result of postponement of consumption.

The production potential measure, thus enlarged, becomes a production-cum-exchange potential measure. The extension is clearly necessary. The possibility of welfare afforded by given resources and techniques depends also on the scope for improvement through exchange with other economies.

III. TRADE IMBALANCE AND THE MULTIPLIER ANALYSIS

While in regard to the analysis of the gains from trade and comparisons of real national income, money flows in foreign trade have been excluded, disproportionate importance has been attached to them in employment theory. The effect of foreign trade on national income and employment has usually been discussed in terms of the multiplier analysis. This analysis assumes that foreign trade is neutral in relation to incomes when there is money balance and that a money export is deflationary while a money import is inflationary. The various foreign-trade multipliers take account of the relationship between exports, imports and income in money terms([2], [8], [9].)

The theory of the multiplier as originally stated by Professor Kahn[5] was in real terms. It measured the relationship between the number of workers employed on investment and the final increase in employment. The corresponding money-income multiplier would have been obtained by weighting each unit of labour by the wage at which it was employed. Keynes' multiplier in *The General Theory of Employment Interest and Money* was also ostensibly a real multiplier because it was in terms of wage-units. This is, however, a money multiplier, because no adjustment is made for the effect of changes in the wage-unit over the period on the relation between money investment or income and real investment or income. The method of conversion from money terms to real terms would be to apply the change in the wage-unit as deflator. The same deflator would be applied to both income and investment, and the result would be identical with that obtained with adoption of money values only. It is necessary for adequate deflation that the period taken be broken up into sub-periods in each of which the wage-unit is constant and the amounts of income and investment in money terms be converted into wage-units for every one of the sub-periods. The ratio of the total of income in wage-units so calculated to the total of investment in wage-units would give a real multiplier. Many of the later multipliers suggested do not approximate even to the extent of the *General Theory* multiplier to real terms.

In relation to a closed economy, the limitations due to inadequate deflation are not as serious as when foreign trade enters the picture.

In the case of a closed economy, there is at least no doubt as to whether investment or dis-investment has taken place over a period. In the case of foreign trade, even the direction of the effect on income may be affected by the absence of deflation or by unsuitable deflation. Imports provide an off-set to exports, and it is the balance that is significant. Should the real balance have a different sign from the money balance, the effect on money income and on real income of foreign trade may be in opposite directions.

This point may be illustrated by a numerical example. Assume that during the year under consideration the price of the wage-unit, used as deflator, increased at the end of the first six months. If imports are concentrated in the first half of the year and exports in the latter half of the year, it is possible that a money export surplus will be accompanied by an import surplus in real terms.

Period	Money exports	Money imports	Money balance	Wage-unit price	Real exports	Real imports	Real balance
1st half	40	50	−10	1	40	50	−10
2nd half	60	36	+24	3	20	12	+8
Total	100	86	+14		60	62	−2

The deflator problem is clearly of significance. Keynes adopted the wage-unit in the *General Theory*. In view of the 'money illusion', this is likely to be 'stickier' than most price indices. This is particularly so in relation to foreign trade. In the domestic field an increase in money investment and incomes which raises prices is likely to lead to at least some increase in money wage-rates and the real income multiplier with wage-unit deflator is likely to be smaller than the money income multiplier, even if larger than the real-income multiplier with wholesale-prices deflator. The wage-unit may, however, not vary at all in response to changes in export and import prices. Thus, a fall in import prices may be absorbed as an increase in real wages with no change in money wage-rates, and the wage-unit may not change. On the other hand, there may be 'autonomous' changes in the wage-unit level due to collective bargaining, etc. It would probably be more appropriate to adopt as deflator a whole-sale-prices index or a wage-goods prices index. From the foreign-trade point of view, the wholesale-prices index would be most suitable. It would reflect changes in both export and import prices.

The appropriate weights would probably be shared in consumption and not turn-over; the latter basis would give undue weight to commodities which go through a relatively large number of distributive stages.

The consideration of imbalance in real terms is of significance in relation to the terms-of-trade concept. It would be useful to construct price terms-of-trade indices, taking account of goods and services only, on the basis of a 'real' balance rather than a money balance. The assumption would be that exports are converted into the deflator commodity and the stock used to buy imports, rather than that exports are converted into money and the amount of money obtained is spent on imports. The variation in assumption affects the amount of imports assumed to balance the given level of exports. To obtain the price terms of trade on this basis, deflation will be necessary of the usual price terms-of-trade series by the ratio of the weighted-average deflator prices in regard to exports and imports in the base year or the later year, depending on whether base or later-year quantity weights are used. The Laspeyres and Paasche price terms-of-trade index would be written respectively, as

$$\frac{\Sigma p_1' q_0'}{\Sigma p_1 q_0} \times \frac{\Sigma p_0 q_0}{\Sigma p_0' q_0'} \times \frac{P_0'}{P_0}$$

and
$$\frac{\Sigma p_0 q_1}{\Sigma p_0' q_1'} \times \frac{\Sigma p_1' q_1'}{\Sigma p_1 q_1} \times \frac{P_1}{P_1'}$$

where P_0, P_0', P_1 and P_1' represent the average prices of the deflector commodity in the base year (suffix 0) and in the later year (suffix 1) weighted by the distribution of the flow of exports (indicated by prime) or imports during the period in question.

REFERENCES

[1] G. Haberler, *Theory of International Trade*, English translation, Edinburgh, W. Hodge & Co.
[2] Harrod, R. F., *International Economics*, Welwyn, Nisbet, p. 121.
[3] Hicks, J. R., 'The Valuation of the Social Income', *Economica*, 1940.
[4] ——, 'The Valuation of the Social Income—A comment on Professor Kuznets' reflections', *Economica*, 1948.
[5] Kahn, R. F., 'The Relation of Home Investment to Unemployment', *Economic Journal*, 1931.
[6] Kaznets, S., 'On the Valuation of the Social Income—Reflections on Professor Hicks' articles,' *Economica*, 1948.
[7] Little, I. M. D., 'The Valuation of the Social Income', *Economica*, 1949.
[8] Machlup, F., *International Trade and the National Income Multiplier*, Blackiston & Co., Philadelphia, 1943.

[9] Robinson, J., *Essays in the Theory of Employment*, Oxford, Basil Blackwell, 1953.

[10] Scitovsky, T., 'A Reconsideration of the Theory of Tariffs', *Review of Economic Studies*, 1942.

[11] Viner, J., *Studies in the Theory of International Trade*, New York, Harper, 1937.

13. Optimal Policies to Promote Industrialization in Less Developed Countries[1]

Many of the less developed countries are disillusioned with import-substituting industrialization induced by import duties and controls. High industrial growth rates may be secured without strain on the balance of payments in the early stages of such industrialization, when simpler consumer goods are manufactured. As production of capital and producer goods is taken up, however, the balance of payments becomes adverse. The value of imported industrial inputs as a fraction of industrial output may decline, but the absolute level of these imports rises. Exports of primary products are unlikely to expand at a rate sufficient to pay for the increasing import requirements, except in the case of countries which have the good fortune to own large reserves of materials such as crude oil. This is because the world demand for primary products grows at a rate lower than that for manufactures. As balance of payments strains become serious the rate of growth declines, and even installed industrial capacity may be only partially utilized. Such experiences have led the less developed countries to conclude that they should steadily expand the exports of manufactures as they industrialize, exploiting the comparative advantage in several processed goods which stems from the availability of relatively cheap labour.

Modern theory has in fact established that the levy of tariffs is a sub-optimal means of handling domestic distortions and externalities, or of securing domestic non-economic objectives.[2] If the optimal domestic policy measures are adopted, exports of manufactures will

[1] Jagdish Bhagwati, Mrinal Datta-Choudhuri, R. M. Honavar, Dharma Kumar, I. G. Patel, Richard Portes, T. N. Srinivasan and Paul Streeten provided valuable comments. The views expressed are personal.

not be impeded. Our first object in this paper is to review some of the results proved in this field, and to discuss the disadvantages of using the trade policy measure of multiple exchange rates when domestic intervention is appropriate. In section II we consider situations in which intervention in trade is optimal. We argue further that when import duties are optimally levied to secure revenue, imported inputs used to make exports should be available at world prices; and that taxes on imports for home use will in general be unequal. In the final Section we offer some comments on the trade and aid policies of developed countries.

I

The central point required to be kept in mind when determining the optimal policy to handle a distortion or externality is that intervention should be aimed directly at the point at which the distortion or externality occurs. Similarly, a non-economic objective can most efficiently be secured by a policy measure directly affecting the variable sought to be altered. These rules, which follow directly from modern second-best theory, can readily be applied to determine the optimal policies in various situations. We consider the following cases: (1) The infant industry situation. (2) The existence of a distortionary wage differential between agriculture and manufacturing. (3) The presence of economies of scale. (4) The non-economic objective is to secure a level of output or employment in manufacturing higher than under non-intervention, for example because manufacturing is thought to promote modernization of the society.

The Infant Industry Situation
The infant industry argument for intervention has various aspects, which may be consiered in turn. Unskilled workers entering industry receive on-the-job training in the initial stages. Such training may be general or specific; general training raises the value of the worker to other employers also, while specific training only raises the marginal product of the worker in the firm which provides it. Gary S. Becker [5] has shown that, under competitive conditions, the cost of general training will be borne by the trainees and not the firms. The return on this investment by trainees in themselves will equal the interest rate, given a perfect capital market. Payment for specific training by firms or by workers entails the risk of loss if the employees quit in

the former case or are sacked in the latter; and Becker points out that sharing of costs and long-term contracts are ways of reducing such risk.

In less developed countries the capital market is usually far from perfect. The banks may give loans primarily to industrialists and traders, against the security of stocks of raw materials and finished goods. Workers seeking finance for training may have to rely on money-lenders, who charge higher interest rates in part because, unlike banks, they do not have access to Central Bank refinancing at moderate interest rates. Further, legal procedures for the recovery of unsecured debts may be protracted and ineffective, so that a high risk premium may be charged on loans for training. Workers can of course finance their own training by sacrificing consumption during the training period. They are, however, likely to be willing to do this only if the expected rate of return is substantially higher than the social discount rate, in view of their low incomes. This is why the wages not only of skilled industrial workers, in whose case trade unions can raise wages, but also of carpenters, lorry drivers, tailors, plumbers, nurses and other categories of workers who are often non-unionized in less developed countries may be two or three times as high as those of unskilled labourers. The consequence is that investment in human capital relative to that in physical capital is likely to be too low from the social point of view.[1]

The optimal policy to deal with this distortion is to establish institutional arrangements under which loans to finance training are made available at the social discount rate, and are recovered in instalments over the skilled working life of the borrower. But such institutional arrangements may not be feasible. Then training of that number of workers in each trade should be subsidized which will ensure that wage differentials are at the levels which would prevail if the loan scheme were in operation. There will be excess demand for subsidized training, with those chosen enjoying quasi-rents after securing training.

The emigration of skilled workers, if fixed in supply, entails a loss to those continuing to reside in the less developed country. No doubt, at the margin, a worker's contribution equals his wage, and so *small* emigration inflicts no loss. But *sizeable* emigration of skilled workers

[1] Harberger [11] concludes that in India the return on physical capital is higher than that on human capital. But he considers the return on higher education, and not on vocational training.

in any field reduces output by more than the earnings of these workers. It is however, a mistake, if a longer run view is taken, to treat supplies of skilled labour as fixed. Training can be provided to meet not only domestic but also foreign requirements. When a loan scheme is feasible, the government of the less developed country, and so those continuing to reside in it, can secure a return on the capital invested in emigrants. If unskilled labour is in abundant supply, training people to work abroad may be an attractive investment. It would of course be necessary to take account of political and social problems in the countries of immigration. It must also be kept in mind that highly qualified people with experience may be contributing much more than their wage at home; this consideration, however, hardly applies to freshly trained doctors, teachers, nurses, etc.

Another variant of the infant industry argument is that a pioneer firm in an industry may incur expenditure on acquiring knowledge which is then available free to later entrants.[1] A subsidy to the learning process will be optimal in such a case. Note, however, that the pioneer firm may be able to make other firms pay for the use of the experience it has acquired, either by taking out patents or charging royalties for the supply of know-how; when this is possible, there is no externality justifying a subsidy.

Arrow has shown, in a well-known paper [1], that if productivity in the capital goods industry is a function of cumulative gross investment, then investment will be below the socially desirable level in the absence of intervention. Note that, in this model, the learning process does not take the form of workers making capital goods becoming more skilled over time, with experienced workers commanding higher wages than new entrants to the labour force in the industry. At any given moment in time, the labour force is homogeneous. So there is no externality with respect to the training of labour, which would justify the financing of such training by loan or subsidy. It is assumed instead that if a firm invests more today, the return on any given level of investment undertaken *by any firm* tomorrow will be higher. We have here an externality associated with investment, which justifies an investment subsidy. Bardhan [4] has shown that if productivity rises with cumulative output in an industry, then an output subsidy is called for; in this case the externality relates to

---

[1] Kemp [19] draws attention to this phenomenon and argues that it is likely to justify the levy of a tariff. Johnson [15] and Bhagwati [8] point out that a subsidy to the learning process is the optimal policy in this case.

production. Arrow and Bardhan deal essentially with the same phenomenon as does Kemp in the model discussed in the previous paragraph.

A Distortionary Wage Differential as between Agriculture and Manufacturing

Suppose that land and labour (which are fixed in supply) are used to produce corn and a manufacture under conditions of constant returns to scale and diminishing returns to varying factor proportions, and that while rents are the same in both activities the wage rate is higher in manufacturing because of a distortion.[1] Under non-intervention corn is exported and the manufacture imported. The ratios of the marginal physical products of land and labour will differ in the two activities. There will be a divergence between the product price ratio and the domestic rate of transformation in production. Hagen [12] argued that in these circumstances an import duty should be levied on the manufacture; this would result in more of the manufacture and less of corn being produced. Bhagwati and the present author [6] pointed out that when a factor tax-cum-subsidy cannot be applied to eliminate the distortion, the second-best policy is an output tax-cum-subsidy and not a tariff. The levy of a tariff results in unnecessary welfare loss due to consumers substituting between the goods at other than world prices.

Kemp and Negishi [20] have shown that a minor proposition in [6], that no tariff may exist which is superior to non-intervention, is erroneous.[2] This result may be explained as follows. Suppose that in the initial situation of non-intervention 150 units of corn and 50 units of the manufacture are produced, and that 100 units of each good are consumed. We have chosen units of quantity such that the world price of each good is unity. We now levy a *small* import duty on the manufacture. Output of corn declines to 149 units, and that of the manufacture rises to 51·2 units. 1·2 units of the manufacture can be produced in lieu of 1 unit of corn, for the distortion has resulted in a divergence between the domestic rate of transformation in production and the world price ratio. If consumers could still be confronted

[1] Bhagwati and the present author [6] point out that there are several circumstances under which a wage differential is not distortionary.

[2] Bhagwati, Srinivasan and the present author [9] have discussed the circumstances under which some form of intervention will raise welfare, and the optimal types of intervention to deal with various distortions and externalities.

by world prices, they would clearly be better off, for they would now be able to buy 200·2 units instead of 200 units of corn and/or the manufacture at the same price ratio. Assume that if this were the case 100·1 units of each good would have been bought. The tariff in fact raises the relative price of the manufacture confronting consumers; and so say 100·09 units of the manufacture and 110·11 units of corn will be consumed. This *small* shift in the pattern of consumption, however, does not reduce welfare. The value to consumers of the 0·01 units of corn consumed additionally and of the manufacture forgone must be evaluated at the pre-tariff prices—the rise in the price of the manufacture can be neglected as it is small. As the pre-tariff prices are the world prices at which goods are exchanged in trade, the gain and loss cancel out—the values to consumers of the increase in corn consumption and the fall in the consumption of the manufacture are in each case virtually 0·01. The point is that the levy of a small tariff inflicts no consumption cost,[1] while its effects on production are beneficial; and so it raises welfare. Thus some tariff exists which is superior to non-intervention; the levy of a tariff is, however, inferior to that of an optimal production tax-cum-subsidy.

Economies of Scale

A traditional argument for protection of manufacturing is that increasing returns to scale are likely to obtain in this sector, whereas agriculture will probably be carried on under conditions of diminishing returns to scale. Even granted these assumptions, increasing marginal costs of transformation in production may prevail; and if so non-intervention is the optimal policy. If, however, there are decreasing marginal transformation costs, the optimal policy instrument is intervention in production and not a tariff. The levy of an optimal production tax-cum-subsidy may well result in the export of manufactures which may be imported under non-intervention.

Non-economic Objectives

A country may have the non-economic objective of securing more output or employment in manufacturing than would prevail in the absence of intervention, for example because it is thought that industrialization promotes modernization of the society. It will never be sensible to secure such domestic non-economic objectives by

---

[1] The production and consumption costs of a tariff are elucidated by Johnson [13, 14].

I

intervention in trade. The optimal policy will be to direct a subsidy towards that variable whose value is sought to be raised above the laissez-faire level. The industry or industries chosen for intervention must be such that the welfare cost of intervention is minimized.[1]

Suppose that, in the absence of intervention, corn alone is produced, and that not only corn but also imported bicycles and sewing machines are consumed. It is desired to secure specified output at world prices of bicycles and/or sewing machines. The production of bicycles and sewing machines requires domestic labour and imported steel. Corn is produced with labour, land and imported fertilizers, land being a free good.[2] The world price of a unit of each tradeable is unity. In order to avoid consumption loss, consumers must substitute between the three goods at world prices. Any given number of workers growing corn for export earn the most net foreign exchange when technique is such that the marginal value product of fertilizer equals its world price; and so this technique is optimal. The wage rate will then be at the free trade level.

The same technique must be applied in growing corn for the home market. For if the fertilizer–labour ratio is higher (lower) in the production of corn for home use than in production for export, it will be possible to secure more corn, without using more labour or fertilizers, by shifting fertilizers (labour) to export production and labour (fertilizers) to production for home use.

Now suppose that sewing machines are made to meet the output constraint. The optimal technique will be such that the ratio of the marginal physical products of labour and the imported input is the same in making sewing machines as in growing corn. For suppose that this technique has been adopted, and we now consider moving one worker from producing sewing machines to growing corn for export. This worker can earn additional net exports just sufficient to finance steel imports worth his wage at world prices. But this is the quantity of steel required to maintain sewing machine output at the specified level, given the technique we have indicated to be optimal. So it will not be possible to meet the output constraint, while raising

---

[1] Bhagwati and Srinivasan [7], Bhagwati [8], Corden [10], and Johnson [13, 15] discuss the optimal means to achieve various non-economic objectives, when all inputs are domestic. We discuss below the case in which an imported intermediate good is used in production.

[2] The assumption that land is a free good makes it possible to ignore scale factors.

consumption levels, by any reallocation of factors. In order that the optimal technique may be adopted in sewing machine manufacture, *entrepreneurs* in this industry must be confronted by the same relative price of the imported input and labour as those in agriculture. This can be ensured by making steel available to the sewing machine industry at the world price, for the wage rate will be the same in both activities. At these factor prices, the unit cost of a sewing machine will be greater than unity, given our assumption that it is not worth while to make sewing machines under non-intervention. An output subsidy must be provided to make supplies available to consumers at the world price of unity.

Similarly, if it is bicycles that are produced, the optimal technique must again be such that the ratio of the marginal physical products of labour and the imported input are the same as in growing corn. Steel should be made available at the world price; and the difference between the unit cost of bicycles and their world price should be covered by an output subsidy.

Which good should be made to meet the output constraint? The answer is that it should be the good for which unit cost is less, given the optimal techniques and factor prices that we have specified. For if 100 units of either good are to be produced, and the unit costs of bicycles and sewing machines are 1·25 and 1·50 respectively, then foreign exchange will be available to import 25 additional units of sewing machines and/or bicycles if bicycles and not sewing machines are made. The optimal policy is to grant a subsidy of 0·25 per bicycle to the output of 100 bicycles.[1]

The non-economic objective may alternatively be the employment of a specified number of workers in making either bicycles or sewing machines. Once more consumers must be confronted by world prices. Technique in growing corn must be such that the marginal value product of fertilizers equals its world price, for the reasons discussed in connection with the output objective.

Suppose that the specified employment is provided in sewing machine manufacture. The quantity of steel used in the sewing machine industry, in combination with the fixed amount of labour, must be such that it is not possible to raise the consumption of sewing machines, while holding that of other goods constant, by

---

[1] See Srinivasan and the present author [23] for an algebraic proof of these results. The exportable is not domestically consumed in that model.

switching foreign exchange outlay slightly to (from) the import of sewing machines from (to) the import of steel to make sewing machines. This condition for optimality is met if the technique in making sewing machines is such that the marginal value product of steel is unity, given that the price of a sewing machine is unity. The marginal value product of labour in the sewing machine industry will be less than the wage rate, which equals the marginal value product of labour in growing corn. This follows from our assumption that it is not profitable to make sewing machines in the absence of intervention; the unit cost of this product will be higher than unity if labour and steel have to be paid the wage rate and a price of unity respectively. The divergence in the ratios of the marginal physical products of labour and the imported input in growing corn and making sewing machines is consistent with optimality in this case because we are precluded by the employment constraint from shifting labour between these activities.

Similarly, if it is bicycles that are made to meet the employment constraint, the optimal technique will be that for which the marginal value product of steel is unity when the price of a bicycle is unity. Assume that, given these techniques and product prices, the marginal value product of labour will be higher if sewing machines are produced. Then this good should be chosen for manufacture. For suppose that 100 workers are required to be employed to make bicycles and/or sewing machines, and that the difference between the values of output and steel used per worker when products and steel are valued at world prices and the optimal techniques are employed is £3 per week in the case of sewing machines and £2 per week for bicycles. Then national consumption at world prices will be £100 per week higher if sewing machines and not bicycles are produced. The difference between the wage rate and the marginal value product of labour in making sewing machines must be covered by an employment subsidy.

This completes our discussion of the optimal policies for dealing with various distortions, externalities and non-economic objectives of a domestic character. We have seen that intervention in trade is not optimal in any of these cases. So we must reject Kaldor's contention [18] that less developed countries should apply multiple exchange rates to promote manufacturing, on learning by doing or distortionary wage differential grounds. It is sub-optimal for consumers to be confronted by a relative price of manufactures higher than the world price ratio. It is also sub-optimal for producers in agriculture to have to export their output at one exchange rate and to import manufactured inputs such as fertilizers at a more depreciated rate; this is likely to retard agricultural development.

II

There are of course valid reasons for intervention in trade. The exercise of national monopoly power is one such; and the levy of an optimum tariff by a less developed country can improve international income distribution. World welfare would be greater, however, if trade were not impeded and international income transfers were made.

If a currency is over-valued and the exchange rate cannot be changed for political reasons, then the grant of a subsidy to receipts and the levy of a tax on payments at a uniform rate can secure an optimal unified exchange rate. The GATT should recognize that if receipts are subsidized for this reason, there is no ground for retaliatory action by other countries.

Other valid reasons for export subsidies are that the private evaluation of risks in exporting may be unduly high, that a firm opening up an export market may build up a reputation for the country's products which other firms can exploit, or that aid flows vary directly with export performance.[1] The central point to be kept in mind is that a distortion or externality must relate to foreign transactions for intervention in trade to be the optimal means of dealing with it.

It may be necessary to levy taxes on trade for revenue reasons, particularly in less developed countries which do not have the administrative means to tax wealth, income and consumption adequately. Srinivasan and the present author [23] have shown that, when trade taxes are levied, inputs used to make exports must be available at world prices, which are assumed to be given. A verbal explanation of the algebraic proof provided in [23] may be of interest. Suppose that imported steel and domestic labour are used to make one good for export and one consumer good for the home market. A second consumer good is imported, World prices are given, as the country has no monopoly power. A specified fraction of the wage bill

[1] See Bhagwati [8, pp. 11–14] and Streeten [24] for a full discussion of these and other arguments for export subsidies.

is required to be collected as revenue. Suppose that initially the revenue constraint is met with steel used to make exports being subjected to tax. Technique in making exports will be such that the marginal value product of steel equals its tax-inclusive price. This determines the wage rate. Technique in making the consumed good for home use is determinate, given the wage rate and the tax-inclusive price of steel for home use. The price of the domestic consumer good equals its unit cost, and that of the imported consumer good equals its world price plus duty. Given balanced trade, and redistribution of tax proceeds to consumers, the quantities of the domestic and imported consumer goods demanded are determinate.

Now remove the duty on steel used to make exports. Technique in export production become more steel-intensive. Assume that as a result the wage rate rises by 10 per cent. We now increase the duty on steel imported to make the domestic consumer good so as to increase its tax-inclusive price by 10 per cent, say from 20 per cent to 32 per cent. So technique in making this good is unchanged, and its price rises by 10 per cent. We further raise the duty on the imported consumer good so as to raise its cost to consumers by 10 per cent, say from 40 per cent to 54 per cent. Consumers are now confronted by the same relative price as before.

Suppose that the allocation of labour between production for export and for the home market remains unchanged. Each worker producing exports earns more net foreign exchange, for the net foreign exchange earned per worker in export production is maximized when technique is such that the marginal value product of steel equals its world price. The quantity of steel required to make the domestic consumer good is the same as before, for employment and technique in this industry are unchanged. So foreign exchange is available to raise supplies of the imported consumer good, while holding constant the supply of the domestic consumer good. By shifting labour from the export industry to the domestic consumer good industry, it will be possible to increase supplies of the domestic consumer good while reducing the increment in the supplies of the imported consumer good. If neither good is inferior, consumers will in fact want to consume somewhat more of both goods at a constant relative price. As the prices of both goods have risen in the same proportion as the wage rate, total consumer expenditure will have increased in at least the same proportion. As tax revenue is simply the difference between total consumer expenditure and the wage bill, it rises proportionately more than the wage rate; and the revenue constraint continues to be met. The point is that the taxation of export inputs inflicts a production cost without reducing consumption cost; and so taxation is not optimal.

Srinivasan and the present author [23] have also shown that in general duties on imports for home use will not be uniform in the second-best revenue tariff. The conventional wisdom of the international economic institutions is that a uniform duty on imports for home use is optimal because it equalizes the marginal utilities derived from alternative uses of foreign exchange. This argument is erroneous because it is based on the false implicit assumption that the allocation of domestic factors to export production, and so the availibility of foreign exchange to finance imports for home use, are invariant with respect to tax rates. Consider a model simpler than that in [23], in which corn alone is produced by domestic land and labour, whether under free trade or after levy of a tariff, while corn and imported sewing machines and bicycles are consumed. The world prices of a unit of corn, a sewing machine and a bicycle are given and are unity. The output of corn is always 200 units. Trade is always required to be balanced. Under free trade, 150 units of corn are exported; and 50 units of corn, 75 sewing machines and 75 bicycles are consumed. We now wish to collect 5 per cent of domestic factor incomes as revenue for redistribution to consumers. Suppose that this revenue constraint is met when a 10 per cent duty is levied on imports of sewing machines and bicycles, with 100 units of corn, 75 sewing machines and 25 bicycles being consumed. We now lower the duty on sewing machines to 9·99 per cent and raise that on bicycles to 10·01 per cent. Suppose that as a result 99 units of corn, 77 sewing machines and 24 bicycles are consumed, the export of corn rising from 100 to 101 units. The revenue constraint is more than met. Welfare is also higher; for while consumers have foregone one unit of corn and one bicycle whose worth to them is 1·0 and virtually 1·1 respectively, they are consuming additionally two sewing machines whose value is virtually 2·2. The point is that the switch to non-uniform tax rates has resulted in a shift of consumption from the exportable, whose value to consumers is its world price, towards an importable which is worth significantly more than its world price because of the tariff.

The uniform tariff of 10 per cent can be optimal only if a slight increase (decrease) in the duty on sewing machines and a slight decrease (increase) in the duty on bicycles, which result in the revenue constraint continuing to be met, leave corn consumption and exports at their previous levels. In that case, the values to consumers of the changes in the quantities consumed of sewing machines and bicycles will be equal, and welfare will not improve. This is obviously a special case. In general, uniform duties on imports for home use will not be optimal, even if these imports are only of final consumer goods. It has been shown in [23] that such uniform duties on imports for home use will on some assumptions be sub-optimal, when these imports are of an intermediate good and a final consumer good.

III

We have shown that less developed countries should apply domestic policy measures to handle various distortions, externalities and non-economic objectives which are often held to justify protection. The main valid reasons for intervention in trade are the need to collect revenue and the exercise of national monopoly power when aid flows are inadequate.

The rich countries have administrations which can tax income, consumption and wealth effectively. It is unlikely that taxation of imports is an optimal means of raising revenue in these countries. The exercise of national monopoly power by the rich nations worsens international income distribution and so cannot be justified. The developed countries should therefore unilaterally dismantle trade barriers. As Thomas Balogh [2, 3] has so often pointed out, tariff reductions based on reciprocity are necessarily biased against the less developed countries. For these less developed countries have less to offer in negotiations, and are, unlike the developed countries, justified in levying tariffs to collect revenue and to exercise national monopoly power. Reciprocity is meaningless in the relations between unequal partners.

The aid policies of rich countries must also be such that the less developed countries can develop adequately and steadily while exploiting trade possibilities fully. The use of aid to promote political objectives, abrupt reductions in aid flows as an easy means of handling balance of payments difficulties, aid financing only of purchases made in the donor country, insistence that aid should be used to purchase complete equipment for projects in the mistaken belief that capital formation in the recipient nation is thereby promoted, and earmarking of aid funds for particular commodities to promote the interests of individual suppliers are examples of policies of donors that encourage the adoption of autarkic policies in less developed countries as a means of reducing political embarassment and economic risks.

REFERENCES

1. Arrow, K. J., 'The Economic Implications of Learning by Doing', *Review of Economic Studies*, Vol. XXIX, June 1962, pp. 155–73.
2. Balogh, T., *Unequal Partners*, 2 vols, Oxford, Basil Blackwell, 1963.
3. Balogh, T., *The Economics of Poverty*, London, Weidenfeld & Nicolson, 1966.
4. Bardhan, P. K., 'On Optimum Subsidy to a Learning Industry: An Aspect of the Theory of Infant-Industry Protection', mimeographed, 1966.
5. Becker, G. S., 'Investment in Human Capital: A Theoretical Analysis', *Journal of Political Economy*, Vol LXX, Supplement: October 1962, pp. 9–49.
6. Bhagwati, J. and Ramaswami, V. K., 'Domestic Distortions, Tariffs and the Theory of Optimum Subsidy', *Journal of Political Economy*, Vol. 71, February 1963, pp. 44–50. Reprinted in R. E. Caves and H. G. Johnson (eds), *Readings in International Economics*, published for the American Economic Association by Richard D. Irwin, Inc., Homewood, Illinois, 1968, pp. 230–9, Also reprinted in Bhagwati, *Trade, Tariffs and Growth*, Weidenfeld & Nicolson, 1969. This constitutes chapter 1 of the present volume.
7. Bhagwati, J. and Srinivasan, T. N., 'Non-Economic Objectives and Optimal Policy Intervention', *Review of Economic Studies*, Vol. 36, January 1969, pp. 27–38.
8. Bhagwati, J., *The Theory and Practice of Commercial Policy; Departures from Unified Exchange Rates*, Princeton University, 1968.
9. Bhagwati, J., Ramaswami, V. K. and Srinivasan, T. N., 'Domestic Distortions Tariffs and the Theory of Optimum Subsidy: Some Further Results', *Journal of Political Economy*, Vol. 77, November/December 1969, pp. 1005–10. This constitutes chapter 2 of the present volume.
10. Corden, W. M., 'Tariffs, Subsidies and the Terms of Trade', *Economica*, NS, Vol. 24, August 1957, pp. 235–42.
11. Harberger, A. C., 'Investment in Men versus Investment in Machines: The Case of India', in C. Arnold Anderson and Mary Jean Bowman (eds), *Education and Economic Development*, Chicago, Aldine Publishing Co., 1965, pp. 11–23.
12. Hagen, E. E., 'An Economic Justification of Protectionism', *Quarterly Journal of Economics*, Vol. LXXII, November 1958, pp. 496–514.

13. Johnson, H. G., 'The Cost of Protection and the Scientific Tariff', *Journal of Political Economy*, Vol. 68, August 1960, pp. 327–45.
14. Johnson, H. G., 'Tariffs and Economic Development: Some Theoretical Issues', *Journal of Development Studies*, Vol. I, October 1964, pp. 3–30.
15. Johnson, H. G., 'Optimal Trade Intervention in the Presence of Domestic Distortions', in R. E. Caves, H. G. Johnson and P. B. Kenen (eds), *Trade, Growth, and the Balance of Payments; Essays in Honour of Gottfried Haberler*, Chicago, Rand McNally and Co., 1965, pp. 3–34.
16. Johnson, H. G., 'A Theoretical Model of Economic Nationalism in New and Developing States', in H. G. Johnson (ed.), *Economic Nationalism in Old and New States*, Chicago, University of Chicago Press, 1967.
17. Johnson, H. G., *Economic Policies Toward Less Developed Countries*, Brookings Institution, Washington D.C., 196 .
18. Kaldor, N., 'Dual Exchange Rates and Economic Development', in his *Essays on Economic Policy*, Vol II, London, G. Duckworth and Co. Ltd., 1964, pp. 178–200.
19. Kemp, M. C., 'The Mill-Bastable Infant-Industry Dogma', *Journal of Political Economy*, Vol. 68, February 1960, 65–7.
20. Kemp, M. C. and Negishi, T., 'Domestic Distortions, Tariffs and the Theory of Optimum Subsidy', *Journal of Political Economy*, Vol. 77, November/December 1969, pp. 1011–13.
21. Meade, J. E., *Trade and Welfare*, Oxford University Press, London 1955.
22. Meier, G. M., 'Free Trade and Development Economics', in J. N. Wolfe (ed.), *Value, Capital, and Growth. Papers in honour of Sir John Hicks*, Edinburgh, University Press, 1968, pp. 385–414.
23. Ramaswami, V. K. and Srinivasan, T. N., 'Optimal Subsidies and Taxes when Some Factors are Traded', *Journal of Political Economy*, Vol. 76, August 1968, pp. 569–82. This constitutes chapter 4 of the present volume.
24. Streeten, P., 'The Case for Export Subsidies', *AICC Economic Review*, Vol. 14, April 1963, pp. 15–16.

14. The Promotion of Industrial Development

This paper is based on my experience as an official economist concerned with problems of industrial development in India. Much of what I have to say may not be applicable to other developing countries, or may be applicable only with qualifications. The conclusions that can be drawn from Indian experience may, however, be of some general interest, in view of the considerable industrialization that has taken place in India over the last decade.

The existence of a large surplus labour force in agriculture is the main reason for industrialization in India. Whether or not the labour force in agriculture is so large that the removal of some workers from the land will have no effect at all on output, it is clear that reasonably productive employment cannot be provided for additions to the labour force without a rapid expansion of industry.

Industrialization is also called for in India on balance of payments considerations. Exports cannot be a leading growth sector. The rate of increase of population is such that agriculture cannot contribute large surpluses for export even allowing for improved productivity per acre. The world demand for the major export items—jute, textiles, cotton textiles and tea—cannot be expected to increase rapidly. Iron ore is the main commodity which is being exported in substantial quantities and has a good growth potential. Indian planning has therefore been directed primarily to the production of the articles on which increased incomes will be spent. The additional consumption from higher incomes is directed largely to industrial products, such as textiles and bicycles. The expansion of agricultural output requires larger quantities of industrial inputs such as fertilizers and pesticides. As incomes rise, the proportion saved will increase; and the investment goods bought with savings, such as tractors, implements and machinery of various kinds, must again be provided by industry. The growth rate of industrial output has therefore to be well above the rate of increase of national income as a whole.

In Indian planning, there are fairly detailed projections of the pattern of industrial development for a period of years. Such projections have been found to be of value in securing the right investment decisions, as they point up the areas of growing demand. Forward estimates for a number of years do, of course, require periodic revision, and there is an elaborate machinery for consultation between industry and government to review progress and revise investment programmes from time to time. The existence of a detailed programme is nevertheless of considerable value; when the pattern of demand is changing rapidly, individual businessmen cannot foresee requirements with certitude in the absence of such an overall picture.

The industrial programme also provides the basis for planning of basic facilities, such as power, water and rail transport. Careful matching of supplies and demands is necessary to avoid significant under-utilization of capital equipment either in power plants and the railway system or in industry. Another objective of industrial planning is to match the expansion of capacity in processing industries with the growth in supplies of basic materials, such as steel; with a difficult balance of payments situation, expansion of imports to make up for short-falls in domestic supplies of raw materials may not be feasible.

When imports are severely restricted, it is easy for high cost industrial capacity to be established. Businessmen may assume that protection will continue indefinitely. They may, for example, set up unduly small units, because of lack of finance and a desire to avoid the risks associated with trying to secure too large a share of the market. The political desire to avoid monopolies and to distribute industry regionally may also lead to pressures on official licensing authorities to promote the setting up of unduly small units. Monopoly cannot, of course, be effectively countered by these means; if the total demand for a product is limited there can be only a few units even if each one is small and there will not be effective competition between them. The claims of regions for a share in industrial development of each single industry can be met without setting up eneconomic units. It is now generally agreed in India that capital must be used in the most effective way, and that industrial licensing policy must be directed to secure this.

The charging of an adequate interest rate for capital is one way of ensuring that it is put to the best use. Over the last few years, interest rates have been steadily raised in India. Even so, market prices may not adequately reflect the shortage of capital in relation to labour. Prevailing wage rates probably exaggerate the social cost of labour. It is therefore sensible to use labour rather than equipment for many construction jobs even if costs at market prices will be lower with the mechanized technique. The weaving of cotton textiles is another field in which labour-intensive methods are extensively employed for this reason.

Not only costs but also prices must reflect the scarcity of capital. It is sometimes believed that essential products, and particularly the services provided by public utilities, must be cheap. There is little to be said for this view. The low pricing of essential products can only retard the expansion of supplies, as a result of lack of resources for re-investment. Such supplies as are available are liable to be used in wasteful ways. The extent to which a system of direct controls can secure the allocation of scarce supplies of essential materials to priority uses is limited. Such direct controls will be necessary in temporary situations of imbalance between demand and supply; but the expansion of output on the basis of a price which will secure an adequate return can be the only long-run answer consistent with efficiency.

If industrial projects are to be undertaken at least cost they must be well conceived. The shortage of properly prepared projects is a major limit to development. Quite often, the absence of adequate knowledge about natural resources hinders the preparation of investment plans, The first step is to have reasonably complete surveys of geological resources, meteorological records, etc. Public sector investment in the proving of limestone deposits is a pre-requisite for the rapid growth of the cement industry, and the mapping of iron ore areas must precede the growth of a steel industry or of export of ores. The rapid expansion of these activities is being given high priority in India.

The next step is the preparation of feasibility studies, covering both economic and technical aspects. The working up of detailed project reports will follow the evaluation of the feasibility studies. The lack of facilities for undertaking work of this kind limits the pace of industrial development, and results in the wrong projects being taken up. Foreign firms can, of course, be commissioned to do individual studies. This is, however, expensive, and costs foreign exchange. A foreign firm may also not take fully into account the special circumstances of the economy of the developing country; for example, it may not be able to identify fully local sources of equipment supplies and it may tend to recommend unduly capital intensive methods. The development of skills within the developing country for the preparation of feasibility studies and project reports will therefore be of considerable value. This is a field in which foreign collaboration can be useful. A foreign firm could set up business in the developing country on the understanding that it will employ and train local men. The larger private industrial undertakings in growing industries might set up their own units, and so could the public sector departments or undertakings concerned not only with industry but also with irrigation, mining and transport.

The financial institutions of aid-giving countries have done much to raise the standards of project preparation, by insisting on properly worked up project reports before granting loans. A problem that has, however, arisen in this context is that a financial institution in a developed country normally insists on a project report prepared by its own nationals. A degree of internationalization may be helpful. The detailed work on equipment supplies must naturally be tailored to the source of equipment; but this need not apply to all the stages of the preparation of the detailed project report.

The local financial institutions in developing countries have also, by insistence on properly worked up projects, done much to improve standards. When such a local institution works in co-operation with a lending institution in a developed country, the task of project appraisal can be handled primarily by the former agency on behalf of both, with considerable saving in time and effort.

The financial institutions can often help businessmen to prepare a worthwhile project, and an application which is initially unacceptable may be put into proper shape as a result of such assistance. However, the institutions are primarily concerned with the appraisal of projects submitted to them; and other agencies must assist businessmen in preparing the projects.

Both international and national assistance could usefully be devoted to a somewhat greater extent than in the past to the development of facilities for the preparation—and the appraisal—of worthwhile industrial development schemes in the developing countries.

The easy availability of suitable sites is necessary for the speedy implementation of projects. The supply of developed sites, with buildings, water and power laid on, has been a useful means of stimulating small industry development in India. For the larger industrial units, some fairly quick means of securing land at reasonable prices is essential. The compulsory acquisition of land by government, at somewhat more than the value for agricultural purposes, and transfer to industrial undertakings can provide a solution. If this is not done, the need to negotiate with a large number of small land owners can seriously delay the setting up of industrial projects. Even if negotiations are successfully completed, there can be doubts with regard to titles to land, which may impede the creation of mortgages to secure loans. The compulsory acquisition of land by government can eliminate these difficulties; for this to be politically acceptable, there must be not only adequate compensation but also resettlement of those affected.

It may be difficult for industry to secure a stable labour force, even if there is considerable unemployment. Industrial centres often draw labour from far away, though there is surplus labour in the surrounding countryside; social and cultural factors may account for the unwillingness of the local population to take up industrial employment. The textile mills of Bombay, for example, have a considerable number of workers from north India. The immigrant workers may not bring their families with them and may keep their connections with their villages. The consequence of this is likely to be considerable turn-over of the labour force. While labour of this kind may be nominally cheap, it is difficult to develop skills and raise productivity. The provision of housing, of fringe benefits related to length of continuous service such as pensions and provident funds, and security of employment can help to reduce turn-over. The assurance that the employment will not be terminated, except for reasons of proved misbehaviour or closure of the unit, provides a modern substitute for the security of the joint family. It can have the disadvantage of impairing industrial discipline; whether this happens will depend on the good sense of the unions and of the conciliation and arbitration machinery.

The supply of skilled labour, particularly of the foreman type, can be a major bottleneck. The traditional educational systems introduced by colonial powers in developing countries have often not paid adequate attention to this need. There is likely to be anyhow

141

strong preference on the part of parents and pupils for the more general type of education which can lead up to white collar jobs rather than for training in technical schools. The persistence of relatively high wages for skilled workers can do much to break down this resistance. On the tide of supply, the provision of adequate training facilities for craftsmen, based on an estimate of industrial requirements, must have high priority in the educational programme.

Foreigners may often provide the first industrial managers. In India, British firms introduced modern management in the jute mills and tea gardens of Bengal. The managing agency system provided a means of using a limited supply of foreign managers to run a large number of relatively small enterprises.

Within the developing country, there will often be classes with considerable trading experience. The more enterprising among them —the Parsis and the Marwaris provide Indian examples—may take up industrial ventures. At a later stage of development, the shift to industry of the indigenous trading classes may be more widespread. Traders handling imports may take up manufacture of the products which they distribute, perhaps in collaboration with foreign suppliers. Traders in agricultural produce may set up processing units; the man who instals a rice mill consolidates his hold on the supplies of paddy and the movement of rice from the area. The larger land owners may also take part in this activity.

To a limited extent, men with professional training, such as engineers, may set up small industrial units. Whether they can do so will depend largely on the availability of finance from institutions; professional knowledge, the desire to set up industrial units and possession of capital may not go together.

The main source of managerial ability is likely to be the large or medium corporate enterprise. The growth of such enterprises results in a supply of professional managers from among the educated who want salaried employment. Traditionally, such men would enter the public service or the law. Careers with companies can become an acceptable alternative, if selections and advancement are recognized to be on the basis of merit.

Initially, it may be the foreign companies which provide such openings. They offer greater security, being well established, and their salary levels are likely to be higher, as these need to be attractive to expatriate personnel. Foreign firms may be under political pressure to reduce the number of expatriate officers. It is in any case cheaper to employ local personnel and while foreign firms will naturally wish to have a limited number of expatriate managerial staff, apart from technicians, a steady increase in the proportion of posts held by the nationals of the developing country can be expected.

Many of the locally-owned firms may be family businesses, which do not provide careers for able outsiders. As industry expands, however, some of these firms may change their character. There may be considerable public holding of the equity, and while members of the controlling families may continue to hold directorships and some of the top managerial posts, it may also be possible to others to rise to the highest positions.

The public services may provide a useful source of managerial talent. A considerable number of Indians were employed in senior managerial posts in the railways long before similar opportunities were available in industry, and railway officers have played a useful part in the management of some of the new industrial undertakings. Some general administrators may also have the aptitude for industrial management. In general, however, the public sector enterprises will need to build up cadres of managers, by providing the requisite training and experience on the job.

The development of a large professional managerial class is critical for successful industrialization. Persuading foreign firms to train nationals, encouraging indigenous enterprise to rely more and more on professional executives, and appointing specialists rather than general administrators to run public sector undertakings, can be useful measures of public policy.

Capital is scarce in developing countries, relative to labour and possibly land. The proportion of incomes saved is low, and the mobilization of savings for productive purposes is difficult. This can be partly achieved through taxation. Industrialization itself helps the process. Additional incomes are more likely to be spent on industrial than on agricultural products, and indirect taxes on industrial consumer goods are a very convenient means of taxing the income increases resulting from development. Direct tax yields are also likely to be related more to industrial output than to the national income, and if industry grows faster than output as a whole, tax revenues may rise steadily as a proportion of national income without any increase in rates of tax. In addition an effort should be made to tax specifically those farmers who benefit substantially

143

from development expenditures, through the imposition of betterment levies, for example.

In Indian experience, both life insurance and small savings can be expanded very rapidly, not only in the towns but also in the rural areas. The setting up of organizations for this purpose is well worthwhile, as widely dispersed savings cannot otherwise be mobilized for productive purposes.

The supply of equity capital to industry presents special problems. Personal savings invested in family businesses may suffice for small industries. The large and medium industrial units, however, need a well-established stock market. Initially, the middle classes may be unwilling to assume the risks associated with industrial investment, and even if there is a stock market, the shares of joint stock companies may in fact be held by controlling families. As, however, there is experience of industrial undertakings making profits and providing capital appreciation on shares, a wider public may be interested; and the new managerial class engaged in industry will be a major source of finance. The available evidence indicates that, over the last decade or two, there has been a very considerable increase in India in the number of people investing in equities.

As prevailing interest rates are generally high, dividend rates must be in line, and the proportion of profits ploughed back may be less than in developed countries. The tradition of relatively liberal dividend distributions can set a limit to the financing of expansions from own funds. Discrimination in the tax system in favour of ploughed-back profits can be of help. Such a provision can also be defended on the ground that while the taxation of consumption must be high and progressive on grounds of equity, there must be incentives for investment and savings.

Specialized financial institutions will be needed to supplement the stock market. They can serve as agencies for the transfer of government budget surpluses, or of government borrowings, to private industrial purposes. They can also raise capital from other financial institutions, such as banks, which may not be willing to lend long-term to industry. Unit trusts can make it possible for the small investor to invest in equities while spreading his risk.

There is room for specialization as between financial institutions according to the type of activity financed. Lending to small units may usefully be decentralized, and undertaken by small institutions meeting regional requirements. In India, this type of lending is handled largely by State Finance Corporations. The recipients of loans are often likely to be proprietary concerns or partnerships not maintaining systematic accounts. A close degree of supervision over the operations of the borrowers may be called for, and personal knowledge of the borrower may be essential. There is also in India a central corporation lending to small-scale industries, which has concentrated largely on the supply of equipment on hire purchase. Such centralized lending must necessarily be confined to a part of the value of fixed assets, with legal provision for resumption in the event of non-payment of instalments. The lending institutions covering smaller areas can provide assistance more flexibly.

The *modus operandi* of institutions lending to large and medium-scale enterprise will be different. Here it is possible and desirable to insist on properly prepared project reports. The borrowers are likely to be mainly joint-stock companies, and the extent of supervision of operations can be less. These institutions may undertake not only lending but also underwriting, the provision of guarantees, etc.

In the operations of financial institutions, proper prudence must be combined with some risk taking. New entrepreneurs cannot be encouraged unless the institution is reconciled to accepting a loss now and again. Institutions not subject to direct parliamentary control may be more able and willing to adopt such an approach than those which have to defend individual transactions. A major Indian financial institution, the Industrial Credit and Investment Corporation of India, is entirely private, though the government lent it a substantial sum and has a Director on the Board. The Industrial Finance Corporation of India had a large government holding of its equity till recently, and was subject to detailed parliamentary scrutiny of its operations. A development Bank has, however, now been established under the control of the Reserve Bank, and this has taken over the government holding in the Industrial Finance Corporation. The charter of the Development Bank provides for much greater flexibility of operations than was possible for the Industrial Finance Corporation.

A method by which financial institutions can provide flexible assistance is investment in equity. This can help the undertaking to meet its requirements while maintaining a reasonable debt-equity ratio. If all goes well, the institution can secure a return considerably higher than on a fixed interest loan, while if the enterprise is not successful, it will not have to carry a heavy burden of debt-servicing.

145

K*

This has not been attempted so far by Indian financial institutions, except to the extent that shares have been taken up in pursuance of underwriting obligations. The International Finance Corporation and the Commonwealth Development Finance Corporation do, however, invest in this form.

Reference was made earlier to joint evaluation of projects by institutions in the developing and the developed countries. Such joint evaluation can result in the foreign exchange requirements of the project being made available by the foreign institution. The financing institutions in India have also taken foreign exchange loans against foreign official assistance, and therefore they are able to finance both the rupee and foreign exchange cost of a project in a single operation.

There is an important distinction between the terms suitable for lending to individual industrial undertakings and those on which a developing country can afford to borrow abroad. Any really worthwhile industrial undertaking should be able to repay a loan in anything up to twenty years; if it cannot do so, it should not be started at all. On the other hand, the balance-of-payments outlook for a developing country may be such that the repayment of external debt must be spread over a much longer period, if massive borrowing merely to cover debt servicing obligations is to be avoided. When, therefore, official assistance is made available direct to industrial units in developing countries, or to these industrial units through financial institutions, ways and means have to be found of reconciling these conflicting requirements. That part of official aid which goes to this purpose may be short or medium-term, and the balance of aid may be made available to the government of the developing country on much more liberal terms. Alternatively, the industrial undertaking may repay in local currency over a relatively short period, but the repayment to the foreign lenders in foreign exchange by the government may be according to a different schedule.

Not all industrial undertakings need loans to finance their programmes. There may, however, be a requirement of imported equipment; and the imports may have to be financed against foreign assistance or not at all. In such a case, the technique of evaluation and lending by a financial institution is not appropriate. The government will need to take a loan abroad, against which foreign exchange can be sold to the undertaking against payment in local currency.

The government will need to have its own arrangements for scrutiny of the project, to ensure that it makes a worthwhile contribution to the development programme. Such official scrutiny, where provided for under the normal legislative and administrative procedures, would naturally apply also when a financial institution provides a loan.

Private investment from abroad has the advantage of bringing with it the foreign exchange needed to pay for imported equipment. It can thus not only supplement domestic savings, but supply the additional scarce resource of foreign exchange. The returns on private investment must naturally be substantially higher than on official lending. Foreign investment may, however, strengthen the balance of payments, if a substantial part of it is used for the production of exports or for import substitution. Also, to the extent that profits are ploughed back, there will be no current burden on account of remittances.

The attitudes to foreign investment in developing countries are greatly influenced by the pace and pattern of development. When there is little growth, particularly in industry, the image of foreign investment is one of exploitation of limited natural resources, resulting in a remittance burden which is difficult to bear and in foreign domination of economic and perhaps political life. The indigenous business classes may be opposed to foreign investment as taking the cream of a limited market. On the other hand, foreign investment which forms only a part of a rising level of investment in industry, and which assists the local businessmen in taking up new lines of manufacturing and catering to expanding markets may be welcomed.

While the wholly foreign firm will have a role to play in industries with very new techniques, the joint enterprise of local and foreign businessmen is likely to secure greater acceptance in the developing country, and also contribute more to the raising of managerial and technical standards. The association of the general public with joint ventures, or for that matter with industrial units wholly controlled by foreign firms, through participation in the share capital, can do much to promote acceptance and to encourage the habit of investment in equity.

The straight technical collaboration agreement, without any financial participation by foreigners, must necessarily be far more widespread than investment. The technical assistance provided by

147

international institutions and governments can meet only a small part of the need, and the primary reliance must be on commercial arrangements. Governments of developing countries can play a part in ensuring that the terms of these agreements are not unduly onerous. There may be scope for somewhat greater effort than in the past by governments and organizations of industries in developing countries and by international institutions to assist industrial units in developing countries to secure the kind of collaboration arrangements that they really need. The small businessman in a developing country, with perhaps no industrial experience or knowledge of foreign industrial concerns, is at a handicap in negotiating worthwhile arrangements. Investment centres or similar bodies set up by developing countries can be of some help in this regard.

The application of new techniques from abroad will be called for also in the field of marketing. The organization of distribution of traditional products in a developing economy may be both efficient and cheap. The foodgrains trade, for example, is often remarkably well organized. The sale of industrial consumer goods in rapidly increasing quantities, in order to monetize the economy and secure larger supplies of agricultural products for urban consumption will, on the other hand, involve considerable effort. To be successful, the effort will have to be based on detailed study of how incomes are spent and of the reactions of the consumer to additions in income. Sample surveys of consumer expenditure have been made use of for the purpose in India. While these can provide valuable basic information, there can be no substitute for effective marketing organizations which undertake distribution down to the retail level and continually test the market. The big successes in promoting sales of manufactured consumer goods have been achieved by the firms which have invested heavily in such distribution arrangements.

15. Methods of Estimating Foreign Exchange Receipts and Requirements in the Formulation of a Medium-Term Plan

The medium-term development plan must, like a long-term or short-term plan, be framed in such a manner as to secure both internal balance and external balance. The requirement for internal balance is that investment must equal savings, while the requirement for external balance is that foreign exchange receipts and payments must equal, without unplanned variations in debt. At the first stage o planning it is necessary to make realistic projections at the macro level which are consistent with both types of balance.

Overall Balance

In the first round, the level of investment might be projected having regard to the requirements for securing a satisfactory growth rate. The relationship between the level of investment and the growth rate of national income is given by the investment–income ratio. There are well-known statistical pitfalls in computing this ratio, particularly in agricultural economies in which the response of output to any given level of inputs is influenced greatly by the weather. The overall investment income ratio will also depend considerably on the distribution of investment as between sectors; this ratio would for example be considerably larger for the power and rail transport sectors than for agriculture. The computation of the investment income ratio provides, however, a useful first step towards projecting an appropriate level of investment. If, for example, the investment income ratio is $3:1$, an investment rate of 9 per cent of the national income would secure a 3 per cent rate of growth of the national income. The qualifications with regard to possible short term fluctuations in the investment income ratio and the sensitivity of the ratio to the distribution of investment between sectors must, however, be kept in mind.

A domestic savings income ratio must similarly be projected. It is important to consider separately the rates of savings that can be secured on the basis of current policies and the additional savings that that can be mobilized for investment as a result of the adoption of policy measures for the purpose. Past experience with regard to the response of savings to income increases provides a first approximation to the savings ratio that can be projected on the basis of current policies. Further refinements may however be useful even at this initial stage. Savings are made by government corporate bodies and households and the savings propensities may differ quite widely as between these groups. In the case of government, for example, current expenditures may be assumed to grow at a trend rate and the excess of revenues over such expenditures would constitute government savings. The elasticity of revenues with respect to income growth is an important determinant of government savings. The corporate sector may have fairly established norms with regard to the rate of distribution of dividends and the savings rates in this sector is likely to be considerably higher than for households. Finally, in the household sector the distribution of incomes as between urban and rural families may be significant. Aggregation of projections of savings for each of these sectors provides an overall domestic savings income ratio on the basis of current policies. Consideration could then be given to the possibility of improving the savings income ratio by appropriate policy measures. For example, additional taxation would raise the savings ratio if it is assumed that government has a marginal savings propensity of unity while households reduce consumption to some extent when the tax burden on them goes up. After making allowance for feasible policy measures of this kind a savings income ratio can be projected which may be compared to the investment income ratio assumed earlier.

The gap between planned investment and projected domestic savings must be covered by an inflow of foreign capital, if internal balance is to be maintained. A judgement is necessary as to whether the rate of inflow of foreign capital assumed is realistic. Comparison can be made with past levels of inflow of official assistance and private capital but such comparisons are by no means conclusive. The question is whether on the basis of a well thought out plan foreign official agencies and private investors can be induced to provide the level of capital inflow required. This is an issue which is partly economic and partly political in character.

The requirement for external balance is that projected receipts, inclusive of the capital inflow assumed, must equal projected payments. Once more, it is important to draw a distinction between the external payments situation on the basis of current policies on the one hand and the effects of policy-induced changes on the other. The first step must be to project the major categories of external payments and receipts on the basis of current policies. The current situation with regard to policy measures comprises the exchange rate, the broad structure of the import tariff and the general level of intensity of quantitative restrictions on imports. Within this framework, projections can be made in the first round taking account, *inter alia*, of the following categories of receipts and payments:

(1) Exports: Export earnings must be forecast having regard to world demand conditions and supply prospects at home. Considerable material is now available with regard to probable trends in world demand for the exports of the main groups of developing countries (the exporters of petroleum products, the exporters of tropical primary products, the exporters of non-tropical primary products and the semi-industrialized countries exporting simple manufactures in addition to primary products). Projections can be made on the assumption that, by and large, market shares cannot be significantly changed. The projections of aggregate exports so derived can be checked against projections of supplies of exportables; if the growth rate of output of exportables is significantly lower than the growth rate of exports indicated by demand considerations, supply limitations may prevent the targets being realized. Even in this first round two or three import export commodities might be considered individually.

(2) Similar projections must be made for invisible items. Freight receipts and payments can be derived from the trade projections after allowing for utilization of domestically owned shipping, if any.

(3) The servicing of external debt can be projected easily with regard to existing obligations fixed in money terms. Allowance must be made in addition for servicing charges likely during the period of the Plan on fresh debt fixed in money terms. Dividends will need to be forecast on some assumptions with regard to profits in the private sector.

(4) Other invisible items of special importance to the country, for example, tourism or remittances from nationals settled abroad would have to be separately projected.

(5) On the imports side it is useful to draw a distinction between project imports on the one hand and imports of components, raw materials and consumer goods on the other. The imports of project equipment will be determined largely by the size and composition of investment in the Plan. The requirements of components and raw materials must be projected with existing demands as a base and allowing for the changes in requirements resulting from the implementation of the Plan. Among consumer goods, food is likely to require special consideration, both because of its importance to the maintenance of internal stability and the special arrangements for external assistance in this area. With regard to other consumer goods a projection based on the income-elasticity of demand indicated by past trends may suffice.

This preliminary exercise may reveal that by and large external balance will be secured with the posited level of capital inflow, in which case both the internal and external requirements for growth with stability are likely to be met. It is, however, possible that the exercise on the external side reveals a substantial deficit or surplus. In that case, consideration must be given in the first place to the possibility of policy-induced changes in the external payments situation.

Consider first the case in which a projected deficit has to be eliminated. It may be possible to raise the exports target if suitable measures are adopted. We referred earlier to studies indicating growth rates of demand in the world market for various categories of products. Many such studies indicate also the extent to which demand should be responsive to price reductions. While the demand for a broad commodity group, particularly in the area of primary products, may be price-inelastic, the price-elasticities of demand for a particular item (for example, one particular kind of fat) may be highly price-elastic if prices of competing products can reasonably be assumed to remain unchanged or at least to be reduced to a lesser extent. The share of the country under consideration in world markets is also relevant. A country accounting for a fairly small part of world trade in an item can much more easily increase its exports by moderate price reduction than a country which has a large share in world trade. Thus the small country, and the country with a diversified pattern of exports, is much better off from the point of view of possibilities of expanding exports through price reductions than the large country or the country with specialization in a few commodities for export.

If it is supply which sets the limit to export, some rearrangement of the pattern of investment visualized initially, in order to give priority to the export sector, may be of advantage. The additional investment must naturally be directed to the export industries for which foreign purchases can be raised with the least sacrifice in prices.

On the side of imports, the pattern of investment visualized in the Plan will be a main determinant of the level of project imports. A shift in the pattern of investment in favour of the sectors with relatively low requirements of equipment would reduce the import bill corresponding to any given level of investment. The policy instruments available to secure such a shift are numerous, the choice depending on the extent of regulation in the economy. Direct allocations of domestic capital and of foreign exchange for project imports could be altered, or higher import duties could be charged on capital equipment or interest rates could be raised to discourage the use of capital generally.

The requirements of imported components and raw materials can also be adjusted through policy measures. Generally higher import duties, for example, would tend both to encourage the production at home of import substitutes and discourage the growth of the sectors relying relatively heavily on importables. With regard to consumer goods of relatively low priority, it may be wise not merely to charge high import duties but also to tax domestic production, in order to avoid diversion of an unduly large quantum of indigenous materials to such uses.

The opposite problem will arise if the excess of payments over receipts on the basis of current policies is smaller than the quantum of capital inflow assumed. This situation can arise in countries in which there is no foreign exchange problem but a shortage of domestic savings. Corrective policy measures must be applied in the first place to raise the level of domestic savings. An increase in the level of taxation and the development of financial institutions such as Development Banks may be helpful. It may further be necessary to readjust the import programme to provide for absorption of the level of capital inflow assumed. The share in the plan of the projects

153

with relatively high import content may have to be raised. There could be provision also for import of suitable consumer goods on a larger scale.

Statistical Limitations of Overall Projection

There may be practical difficulties in making projections of investment and savings, due to inadequacy of data. Information is more likely to be readily available with regard to the supply of money. Though an investment-savings approach may be preferred on theoretical grounds, the only practical course of action may be to consider whether the Plan is likely to result in a growth in the money supply in line with projected increase in real output or not. The main factors accounting for variations in the money supply are the budgetary operations of the government, the growth of deposits with the banking system and the balance-of-payments surplus or deficit. If the initial situation is one of balance, then the expansion of money supply must be in line with output increases, allowing, however, for additional requirements of money due to growing monetization of the economy. Even if the data required for a consideration of the balance between investment and savings are available, an analysis of the monetary situation provides a useful cross check.

The statistical information needed for an analysis of the type outlined above may be briefly considered. The computation of investment income ratios requires information regarding levels of investment and associated outputs in different sectors. At the macro level, the national income accounts should provide this information. It is necessary, however, to have supplementary detailed information with regard to investment requirements for given outputs in major sectors. The process of development quite often involves major structural changes and ratios derived from historical data cannot be utilized. For example, if development is visualized in heavy industry, the relationships between investment and output applying to the light industry that may have been built up in the past will not be of relevance. It is thus necessary to secure, if necessary from other countries, data regarding the investment requirements for the types of projects visualized and the resulting outputs. The time required to complete projects in each major area must not be overlooked; a major irrigation project may take years to result in higher agricultural production, whereas tanks or wells will yield a much quicker return. Information regarding individual sectors is necessary also for determining the import content of investment.

While savings may appear as a balancing item in the national income accounts, more elaborate information is necessary for the purpose of projections. The estimation of household savings, however, presents difficulties. It may be desirable to undertake sample surveys of the response of savings to increases in income. Such surveys would have to deal separately with urban and rural savings trends, and in addition differentiate between categories of households in each sector. Estimation of corporate savings calls for analysis of balance-sheet data with a view to projecting corporate behaviour with regard to ploughing back of profits. Projection of government savings requires study of trends in public non-development expenditures and of the yields from various taxes. The receipts from income and corporation tax might, for example, be related closely to the growth of manufacturing activities or corporate income, while revenues from individual excise taxes might most appropriately be projected on the basis of production trends for the commodities concerned.

Information with regard to the operation of the banking system, including the Central Bank, provides the basis for analysis of monetary trends. Balance-of-payments projections would indicate the contribution of foreign trade and payments to the internal monetary situation. Balance-of-payments data would be required also for computing the external balance. The statistics regarding budgetary operations would also enter into the picture.

To sum up, the formulation of the medium-term Plan requires, even at the initial stage, basic statistics with regard to government finance, national income, investment and savings and the balance of payments. The organization of the collection of such basic statistics is a necessary prelude to Plan formulation.

Input-output Analysis

At a less aggregative level, an input-output table provides useful information for Plan formulation. Such a table summarizes for a limited number of sectors into which the economy is divided, the relationships between the final products desired whether for home consumption or export and the intermediate goods necessary to secure this basket of final products. The technical relationships specifying the amounts of each input needed for any given output are assumed to be always the same, and this does introduce a degree of arbitrariness. Account cannot be taken of the possibility of varying methods of production to secure a given output at least cost. Nevertheless, the approach is useful in throwing up the implications of alternative sets of targets. The final basket of goods for domestic consumption in say the terminal year of the Plan may be postulated on the basis of the rise in income visualized and the income elasticities of demand for different products. The package of goods needed for export could be arbitrarily assumed and similarly assumptions could be made with regard to the package of imports consistent with external balance being maintained. We then have the package of final goods for domestic production and input-output analysis can indicate the supplies needed to be produced of various intermediate products. The associated requirements can then be computed to arrive at an overall investment income ratio which can be checked with overall projections based on past experience. In this form, there is no particular maximizing operation involved in the use of the input-output technique. A further development would be to consider how output (including output for exports) can be maximized at the end of the planning period (or over the planning period, applying a suitable discount rate) on the assumption of a fixed savings income ratio. With regard to imports there could be an overall value postulated for each year. A computation of this kind would throw up information with regard to the basket of exports which, on the assumption of constant prices, would secure the highest rate of income growth. By and large, the results would indicate that building up of the exports of items with relatively low capital intensity would stimulate the growth rate on the assumption that savings are a limiting factor to development. The practical applicability of the results would depend, however, on actual trading possibilities. It may be that substantial expansion of the exports of such items with low capital intensity may result in a deterioration of the terms of trade. It may be, further, that diversification of the export pattern rather than concentration on a few products with low capital intensity may be desirable from the point of view of reducing risks. Application of the input-output technique with explicit maximization of income growth and with suitable assumptions with regard to the savings rate and the level of capital inflow can, however, result in useful quantification of problems and thus secure more efficient plan formulation. While work on models of this kind is still experimental, the technique is one which may become of increasing relevance ot practical problems of planning.

Sectoral Balance

Once a preliminary view has been taken of the values over the Plan period of the overall economic magnitudes and of a tentative sectoral distribution, detailed work is necessary on targets with regard to more narrowly defined sectors. The preparation of these detailed targets in a consistent way can only be achieved through iteration. On the side of investment, targets for the levels of capacity and production in different sectors at the end of the Plan period, and possibly in one or more intermediate years, would have to be drawn up, keeping in mind the targets for home consumption, tentative views regarding export possibilities and the information available regarding the relative advantages of production at home as against imports. The investment required for achieving each of these targets needs to be computed on the basis of detailed information regarding plant cost and cost of land and buildings. Aggregation would indicate whether the preliminary overall estimate made of investment requirements is realistic. From the point of view of foreign exchange planning, the data regarding the import content of investment for achieving each target is significant. There will be a problem of computation here with regard to materials which are partly indigenous and partly imported. Thus, if the country makes a certain quantity of steel, but imports are necessary in addition, it will not be possible to determine with regard to the expansion programme of, say, the railways alone, the import of steel needed. It will be necessary to tabulate separately the requirements of such items with a view to providing for import, for all projects taken together, of the excess of requirements over domestic production.

Simultaneously, an exercise would be necessary with regard to the break-up of the overall export target. Such an examination would take account, in the first place, of the trends in world demand at constant prices for the item in question. In the case of final consumer goods such as cocoa, tea or coffee, straight computation of income elasticities of demand may provide adequate projections of world consumption. Alternative projections might be made on different assumptions regarding rates of growth of income in principal markets. For intermediate products, a more complex procedure would be necessary. Thus, the forecasting of the demand for iron ore involves assumptions with regard to world steel production; and the demand for steel depends in turn on both the demand for capital goods and for the relevant consumer durables. The projections cannot, further, be based solely on past trends. Account would have to be taken, to the extent possible, of the plans drawn up by the consuming countries, though it may be appropriate to make adjustments to allow for probable failure to achieve targets.

Projections of aggregate world demand for different commodities are particularly important for those items in the world market for which the planning country has a major share. It may not be necessary to undertake any detailed exercise regarding trends in world demand for items in which the country's share in world trade is small. For these latter items, it would suffice if some broad judgement is formed as to whether world demand is likely to expand or contract and, if so, whether at rapid or low rates.

For items in which the planning country's share is large, a further judgement is necessary as to the impact on world demand of given price reductions, and the likely reactions of competing suppliers to a price fall. If world demand is price elastic, and competing countries are not likely to retaliate to price cuts by equivalent or larger price reductions, it may be possible for the planning country to secure significant additional earnings through a price reduction. If, on the other hand, foreign demand is price inelastic and competing suppliers are likely to match price reductions, there may be no gain or even loss from attempting to increase one's share of the market through a price reduction.

In the case of items for which a country's share in world trade is small, a substantial increase in earnings may be possible through quite moderate price revisions. It is, however, necessary to draw a distinction between commodities for which there are no specialized marketing problems and demand is very sensitive to minor price changes on the one hand, and items like machinery for which establishing any export sales will take a considerable period on the other. The sustained export of the more complex manufactured products calls not only for satisfactory prices but also for the provision of adequate after-sales service and the building up of reputation; and these things take time. Even with regard to the simpler items of exports the structural factors must always be kept in mind and policy issues thrown up. Quality control can make a considerable difference to the prices realized for exports; in the case of food products, for example, assurance of compliance with international standards is a prerequisite for expansion of export sales. The availability of information with regard to trends in world markets and new marketing opportunities is of considerable importance. This may be secured partly through governmental agencies but in addition expenditure on marketing service in major foreign markets may yield a high return. The structure of the export trade may also require to be strengthened to cope with a major export drive. It may be necessary to establish new links particularly in non-traditional markets in order to build up exports. The export projections would have to specify the assumptions made with regard to the effects of such organizational improvements.

The restrictive aspects of international trade relations will also be relevant and the possibility of overcoming these must be explicitly considered. Certain international arrangements with regard to marketing of primary commodities set quantitative limits to exports from individual countries. Even when there are not such quantitative limits, the specification of prices could indirectly set a limit to exports. For example, in manufactured items such as cotton textiles, there are agreements restricting world trade. For other simple manufactures, some importing countries impose quantitative restrictions. The restrictions applied on balance-of-payments grounds also tend to be applied to restrict certain categories of imports than others, having regard to the productive capacities in the countries applying the restrictions. Finally, foreign tariffs are a barrier to exports. While initial projections may be made on the assumption that trade barriers will remain unchanged, it is necessary to specify the increments to exports that may be secured through policy changes abroad that appear feasible. The most promising of such policy changes would then have to be negotiated with the foreign countries concerned. Mention may be made in particular of regional co-operation in the reduction of trade barriers as a promising means of expanding trade with benefit to all participant countries.

The domestic policy measures that are necessary to sustain and expand export earnings must also be clearly spelt out with an indication of the quantitative impact on export earnings. The domestic consumption of promising export commodities could be restrained through excise duties. Reference has been made earlier to the desirability of stimulating exports of items with elastic foreign demand price reductions; and a policy of export subsidies for such commodities may be worth considering. While a general reduction in export prices could be secured through an exchange rate change, selective measures would be necessary to take advantage of varying foreign demand elasticities for export products. In the case of manufactured goods, there may be an infant industry argument for export subsidies, on lines analogous to the infant industry argument for protection.

The requirements of 'maintenance imports' components, raw materials, spare parts and consumer goods—can be projected in greater detail in the second round. Consider first the requirements of components and raw materials for the larger items consumed by identifiable and organized sectors of the economy, such as the raw materials needed by large scale industry. The requirements can be estimated on the basis of the full capacity working of industry. The tentative decisions already taken with regard to the projects that are to be established provide an indication of the industrial capacity that requires to be fed during each year of the medium-term Plan; it would be reasonable to assume that, by and large, the maximum number of shifts that is technically feasible will be worked, for it would be wasteful to leave manufacturing capacities even partially idle. Care must, however, be taken to allow a reasonable running-in period for new projects and expansions. Further, allowances must be made for any structural imbalances which exist in the economy and which cannot be corrected over the period of the Plan. For example, capacity may have been built in the past in some industries for the full output of which the demand does not exist at current prices; and there would be no point in providing for the raw materials needed to use such capacity. Allowance must be made also for any major technological changes that are anticipated; for example, if the steel industry uses increased quantities of fuel oil in blast furnaces, the necessary provision for the import of fuel oil must be made. In the case of engineering industries which start with assembling of imported items and gradually increase value added according to phased programmes, the import projections must take account of this gradual reduction in the import content of output. An important point which must not be overlooked is the need to provide for inventories of raw materials to match increases in levels of output. Projections need to be made for raw material requirements of major industrial sectors taking these considerations into account. Deducting anticipated increases in indigenous output of these raw materials, the import requirements can be arrived at.

The requirements of raw materials for smaller units, of spare parts for industry generally and of minor balancing and replacement equipment will have to be estimated less directly. The requirements of such raw materials and spare parts could be projected by taking a base consumption figure and projecting at the growth rate visualized for output in these sectors. The requirements of miscellaneous equipment for replacement and balancing purposes can be estimated by applying a historical percentage to an estimated capital stock in manufacturing industry, making allowance for any bunching of replacement requirements in important industrial sectors. It may be desirable to collect information specifically regarding the age composition of the capital stock. As a matter of policy it may be desirable to allow for replacement after a considerably longer period of use than is customary in developed countries.

While the costs of production and selling prices will have been specifically considered in relation to project possibilities, the scope for minimizing imports through price changes that facilitate the full use of industrial capacity must be given specific consideration when requirements for imports of components and raw materials. There may be possibilities both of substitution of domestic output of a product for imports through tariff protection and of substitution of an indigenous product for a different but competing imported product. For example, if aluminium can be manufactured locally but copper is not, protection of the aluminium industry may result in full use of indigenous aluminium-making capacity at the expense of the imports of aluminium, and in addition the taxation of copper could result in the substitution of aluminium for copper. If import restrictions are maintained for balance-of-payments reasons these could supplement duties in securing import substitution. In other words, infant industry protection need not necessarily be confined to the levy of duties on the specific product being manufactured; it may be desirable to extend the protection to substitutes in consumption.

The import requirements of agriculture—fertilizers, pesticides, implements and so on—also require to be projected taking into account the development programme visualized for agriculture. The technical relationships between inputs of various kinds and the planned outputs of agricultural products would be relevant. It would be necessary to point out the policy implications with regard to official assistance in marketing and in the training of the farmer to use additional inputs. If a major programme to change present techniques of farmers through training and assistance is visualized, market trends can provide relatively little guidance for projections; the latter must be related largely to the development programme designed to bring about structural changes.

In countries importing petroleum products, fuels are likely to be a major area of import. The demand for fuels is partly for transportation, partly for power for agriculture and industry and partly for lighting purposes. The estimation of fuel requirements for transport involves in the first place consideration of the rail and road transport which will have to be undertaken as part of the transport programme. The rail transport system may use partly coal and partly oil whereas the road transport system would depend on oil entirely. Specific consideration of the economics of dieselization of rail haulage would be necessary. Projections of the quantum of rail and road haulage could be used to forecast the demand for oil and coal having regard to the present extent of the use of coal and oil respectively in road transport. Similarly, the scope for use of coal and oil in power generation could require consideration. Requirements for miscellaneous purpose such as lighting and for agricultural pumps could be projected on the basis of income growth in rural areas, and the requirements of the agricultural programme. This is an area in which demands are particularly sensitive to relative prices and if fuel is imported, really detailed consideration of the cost of alternatives would be worthwhile.

Among consumer goods, really careful estimation may be desirable with regard to food imports. This would have to be based primarily on income projections and estimates of income elasticities of demand. The extent of urbanization visualized could also be an important factor. From the policy point of view, there may need to be a specific commitment to feed urban areas at prices which do not rise too sharply, while the commitment with regard to rural areas can only be less definite. In so far as supply to the urban areas is concerned, what is relevant is not aggregate home output imports but the marketed surplus of farmers plus imports; and fluctuations in the marketed surplus will naturally be larger than in agricultural output. Variations in the proportion of rural income spent on food would have a proportionately greater effect on the supplies made available to the towns. Provision would be necessary for stocks to offset such variations as also the variations in production due to weather factors; while a Plan may postulate an increase in output, variations from year to year would be inevitable. The scope for additional food imports and a larger investment programme also requires to be considered; there could be special arrangements for such imports under aid programmes. As far as other consumer goods are concerned, estimation on the basis of past trends after allowing for policy induced measures to restrain consumption may be adequate.

Among invisible items, shipping charges will require specific estimation. Once the quantities of various items of export and imports have been estimated, these can be converted to a tonnage basis. Freight rates will need to be projected and applied to these tonnages. The necessary adjustments must be made to export earnings calculated c.i.f. or import charges calculated on an f.o.b. basis. If the country has any shipping, estimates of earnings must be arrived at. Similarly, adjustment is necessary for insurance charges.

Estimates of remittances on account of profits and royalties can be refined once there are detailed projections of production. Charges on account of royalties may, by and large, be related to production trends in manufacturing and perhaps in mining and petroleum production, with adjustments for any likely variations in the extent of output covered by collaboration agreements. Remittances of profits would depend upon the inflow of private capital assumed, any likely variations in the profitability of industry and the assumed policy regarding plough-back of profits. The projections may throw up a number of policy points for consideration. By and large, remittances on account of profits arising from new projects would start only later than royalty payments related to production; from this point of view it may be desirable to encourage investment rather than straight purchase of know-how. Even where payment is to be made for straight know-how, capitalization of this amount rather than payment in cash would postpone the liability. Further, the interest taken by the foreign collaborator may be greater if there is cash investment. On the other hand, the ultimate servicing burden may be higher in the case of private investment particularly in industries which are likely to earn abnormally high profits; both on this and other grounds it is desirable to ensure through appropriate fiscal measures that products of which the consumption is sought to be restricted on ground of priority are adequately taxed.

The detailed projections in the various sectors of visibles and invisibles can be aggregated and an overall picture obtained of

L

external receipts and payments for purposes of aid negotiations. The payments estimates must be broken down into the project and non-project categories, with an intermediate area consisting of payments related to projects but not directly for equipment. Payments for fertilizers and other requirements of the agricultural programme, or of components and steel needed to manufacture capital equipment within the country provide examples of requirements of development programmes which are not strictly for projects but which could be put together for aid programmes. If the quantum of foreign aid projected is greater than the machinery requirements of projects proper, aid can be absorbed only if available to finance imports for programmes of the type mentioned or as general balance of payments support. Alternatively aid would have to be available to cover the local cost of projects, the foreign exhange counterpart utilized for general expenditures. It may be desirable also to estimate payments to the main countries giving aid, in view of the extensive country tying of aid. Possible sources for each major project would have to be listed in order of priority, the final distribution between countries of projects depending upon the amounts available from each source and the interest of the donor countries in various sectors of the recipient country's economy. Aid available for financing commodity imports may also be country-tied and it would be wise to work out the cost of purchase from alternative sources with a view to making the available foreign exchange go as far as possible. Food would fall in a special and separate category. As and when details become available regarding amounts and sources of aid, the import programme would require readjustment, resources being deployed to secure the most effective use of assistance.

METHODS USED IN COMPLETING BALANCES FOR SPECIFIC COMMODITIES

Steel

The projection of the supply and demand for steel provides a good example of the problems involved in constructing a commodity balance, as this is a raw material entering into many different uses. The methods of a study done in India with regard to steel requirements in 1965–6 and 1970–1 will be used for purposes of illustration.

It has been found that steel consumption has been rising sharply relative to investment and national income in India, in view of the emphasis on the production of engineering goods in the plans. It was, therefore, found necessary to estimate requirements by detailed application of the end-use approach.

In assessing requirements of steel of the industrial sector, three types of demands were taken into account:

(1) Steel consumed in manufacture;

(2) Steel required for construction of plants; and

(3) Steel required to maintain plants.

In estimating the demand for steel for manufacturing purposes, the starting point was the targets of production for 1965–6 as set out in the Third Five Year Plan (1961–6) and preliminary targets worked out for the Fourth Five Year Plan (1966–1) by the Perspective Planning Division of the Planning Commission. These targets cover production in large and medium scale industry and, to an extent, also production in small scale industry. The targets were framed having regard both to the final demand for industrial products and the input and output relationships within manufacturing industry. Thus, the demand figure for trucks was based on an estimate of the transport industry's requirements of trucks for expansion and replacement, whereas the demand for truck wheels was related to the planned output of trucks. It was necessary to estimate norms for steel consumption for the manufacture of each product in the twenty major industrial groups considered. Questionnaires were addressed to more than 500 industrial units to secure information regarding category-wise consumption of steel per unit of end-product. The replies received were analysed and norms were worked out on the basis of average consumption. Problems arose because of expected changes in the product-mix; and separate norms had to be fixed for each category of product of sufficient importance to influence the estimates significantly. To give examples:

(1) The paper machinery industry produces both small plants of up to 10 tonnes capacity per day and large plants of up to 100 tonnes capacity per day. There are separate targets for the two types of plants and different norms were worked out.

(2) In the case of machine tools, the various types and sizes were arbitrarily divided into 'small sizes' and 'medium sizes' and different norms were fixed.

(3) For trucks and cars, norms were worked out separately for each industrial unit.

The norms, when applied to the production levels envisaged, provided estimates of the requirements of each industry, with the category-wise breakdown.

For some small scale industries, detailed information regarding production levels was not available. Factories Act data were used to determine the number of units in existence and production levels were estimated from this information. A few business associations also supplied information regarding steel consumption norms, and requirements were estimated by assuming arbitrarily that output would grow more or less in line with that of the large scale sector. For small servicing units producing replacement parts, etc., the number of units was determined from municipal records and it was assumed on the basis of sample field investigation that general and mechanical engineering workshops consumed one tonne of steel per year while vehicle repair shops consumed about 0·10 tonne per year. It was assumed that the number of such shops would increase by about 50 per cent over a five-year period.

It may be noted that the steel demand for manufacturing was derived on the basis of very detailed industrial targets covering twenty major groups of industries comprising several dozen industries and around a thousand industrial units. Revision of these estimates cannot obviously be undertaken in the same detailed fashion. Periodic revisions of the demand estimate for 1965–6 have taken specific account only of likely variations from planned production levels in major steel using industries, such as automobiles. For other industries, an overall estimate has been made of the extent of production shortfall in relation to the target. When final projections are made of the Fourth Plan industrial targets, together with an annual phasing, the steel requirements will be reworked in detail. In the course of the Plan, however, short-term corrections would have to be made by a short-cut method.

The initial estimates were based on existing techniques. However, studies have separately been undertaken of the possibilities of reducing steel consumption through changes in methods of production. Thus, considerable attention is being given to the use of paper and plastics for packaging instead of tin plate. These studies may result both in modification of certain targets for the Fourth Plan and amendment of the projections of various input requirements. Similarly, the possibilities of reducing steel consumption through use of welding, which in turn requires the production of weldable qualities of sections and plates, are being studied.

The demand for steel for factory construction was estimated on the basis of:

(1) statements of requirements from individual major public sector units, and

(2) the proposed level of investment in the private industrial sector.

The proportion of investment devoted to construction was worked out for a number of industries and the category-wise steel requirements for a given expenditure on construction were also computed. It was thus possible to estimate the amounts of each category of steel needed for a given level of investment in construction.

While metal-based industries provided fairly full information regarding their requirements for maintenance purposes, other industries did not; and projections had to be made on a rough and ready assessment of the maintenance requirements of industry in general.

The overall requirements for industrial purposes having been estimated, an allowance of one month's consumption for production purposes was made to cover increases in stocks.

The steel requirements of the transport and communication sector were considered under the following heads:

(1) Railways.

(2) Roads and road transport.

(3) Inland water transport.

(4) Shipping.

(5) Ports and harbours.

(6) Civil aviation.

(7) Posts & Telegraphs.

We shall consider only the method of estimation adopted for the Railway programme. The demand for rail transport in India is itself determined largely by the size of the steel programme as coal, iron ore and steel account for a large part of the traffic carried. In addition, allowance is made for normal growth in other goods traffic and in passenger traffic. The Railway Plan provides for these requirements, and involves expansion of the stock of locomotives and wagons, track renewal and additions, electrification and dieselization etc. The Railways manufacture both locomotives and wagons, and the steel requirements for such manufacture are provided for, on the basis of consumption norms provided by the locomotive and wagon factories. The steel requirements for the track programme were estimated on the basis of the existing usage regarding the shares of steel, cast iron and concrete sleepers; it was noted, however, that as steel sleeper production was expanded, the consumption of cast iron sleepers could be brought down, and further that concrete sleepers might be used more widely if cost consideratons were to justify this. Provision was made also for the steel requirements for bridges, for the electrification programme (on the basis of both Indian and European data regarding consumption norms) and for construction of buildings of various kinds. Maintenance requirements were projected on the basis of past experience and the growth of traffic.

A problem of some importance in estimating the Railways' steel consumption has been the somewhat uneven distribution of investment over time; expenditures have tended to be concentrated in the middle of a Plan period. A recommendation has been made that the phasing of investment should be altered to provide for a gradual stepping up from year to year so as to avoid uneven demand for steel. The scope for keeping down foreign exchange expenditure on steel and components through a matching of the Railway investment programme with the production plans of the steel plants and of the Railway equipment factories is taken into account in formulating and modifying the Plan targets. The need for such adjustment can become apparent only through the iterative process of making some assumptions with regard to production targets in the first place and computing the requirements of steel, components etc. to achieve these targets.

The requirements of steel for the power programme were estimated by taking targets for power generation in thermal and hydro plants, estimating the steel requirements for standard plant of each type, and computing also the steel requirements for the associated transmission systems. Estimating the steel requirements for irrigation projects presented considerable difficulties, in view of the widely differing steel requirements of different types of projects; the best that could be done was to assume that the relationship between the outlay and steel consumption would remain the same as during the early years of the Third Plan. In the social services field, steel is required primarily for buildings of various kinds, and the public sector requirements of steel for such construction was estimated from the share of past outlays spent on consumption and technical norms. The estimation of steel requirements for private housing involved a considerable degree of guess work; savings data and information provided by municipalities regarding the number of houses added each year provided a starting point, and outlays were projected on the basis of expected trends in savings and the proportion thereof likely to be devoted to house construction. As for the agricultural programme, direct estimates were made on the basis of plan schemes of requirements of steel for construction of warehouses, and of buildings connected with agricultural development. The steel component of private agricultural investment could be estimated only indirectly, on the basis of capital formation data provided by a rural credit survey and projections of rural private incomes and savings. Estimates of current requirements for fencing, replacing steel tyres on bullock carts, etc., were projected on the basis of past consumption data. The steel requirements for manufacture of agricultural implements, tractors, etc., had been accounted for in estimating the requirements for industrial production.·

It was a drawback of the study that no detailed work was done in estimating export possibilities, through investigation of individual markets. World trade trends were reviewed, however, and an *ad hoc* provision was made for exports. The sizeable quantum of exports projected for 1970–1 will need to be backed up by further work on possibilities category-wise and in individual markets.

Aggregation of projections for individual sectors provided an overall picture of demand broken into major categories of steel. This was compared with production projections. For 1965–6, production could be expected only from industrial capacity already set up. Estimates of production could, therefore, be based on the established capacity and assumptions regarding improvement in the use of capacity. As much of the installed capacity was new and plants were still suffering from teething troubles, it was necessary to estimate the rate at which these difficulties would be got over.

Estimation of production in 1970–1 had to be based on the provisional target for the Fourth Plan which itself had been built up on the basis of expected production from individual existing and planned units. Such projections required careful scrutiny of the phasing of construction, running in and raising of production levels to full capacity. The various stages taken into account include preparation

169

of feasibility study, location of a likely source of assistance, preparation of a detailed project report, negotiation of a loan to cover the foreign exchange cost, placing of tenders, construction periods for indigenous and imported equipment, erection time, the period required to develop raw material supplies and the period of production needed to build up efficiency to the level required to secure full capacity output. Projections made after allowing for these factors indicated, for both the years, deficits for certain categories (particularly flat products), and marginal surpluses in certain other categories.

The estimates had been made on the basis of constant prices. In view of the sizeable deficits revealed, the scope for reducing demand through higher prices has received attention. Certain categories of steel have been decontrolled, and producers have put up prices to equate supply and demand. The impact of these price increases has been primarily on sectors such as housing construction considered to be of relatively low priority. Tax rates on other categories of steel have also been raised, particularly on varieties such as tin plate entering into consumption rather than investment. Periodic revision of forward estimates of demand at current prices and of production levels must form the basis for revisions of price and tax policies to avoid windfall profits or undue strain on the control system.

Petroleum Products

Estimation of demand for petroleum products involved greater reliance on overall demand analysis and less on assessment of requirements of individual firms, in view of the very large number of users involved. The following categories of products were considered.

(1) Motor spirit.

(2) Naphtha, virtually the same product technically as motor spirit, but used for industrial purposes.

(3) High speed diesel oil

(4) Low speed diesel oil.

(5) Superior kerosene.

(6) Inferior kerosene.

(7) Lubricants.

(8) Furnace oil.

Information regarding the number of motor cars on the road is available from licensing data. Projections regarding additions to the stock were made on the basis of the production programme of the motor-car industry, it being assumed that imports of complete cars would continue to be negligible. Only a small part of the fleet of trucks uses motor spirit and additions to the stock are also likely to be negligible, in view of the decided market preference for diesel trucks and the standardization of major producers on the manufacture of diesel rather than petrol engines. Allowance was made for the consumption of the small number of petrol trucks.

Naphtha, which is virtually the same product as motor spirit, can be used as a feed stock for the manufacture of fertilizers, petrochemicals, etc. These industries can also be based on coal. Technoeconomic studies have, however, shown that the cost of production of fertilizers and petro-chemicals will be significantly lower if naphtha is used. Allowance was, therefore made for the naphtha requirements to achieve production targets in these industries using naphtha as a feed stock. Further, experience abroad indicates that the output of steel blast furnaces can be substantially increased if naphtha is used; experiments are being conducted in Indian plants and if these prove successful the projections will be revised to provide for larger requirements of the steel plants.

Naptha can be used also for power generation. In areas near coalfields such use of naphtha would not be economic. It is preferable either to move coal to power-stations near consuming areas or to generate power in large power-stations situated near the coalmines and to move the power by transmission lines. In areas distant from the coal-fields, but on the coast or close to indigenous supplies of crude oil, it may, however, be economic to use naphtha as a fuel for power generation. The optimal consumption of naphtha for power generation has thus to be determined on the basis of both overall norms regarding the extent of coal haulage (or power movement by transmission lines) that is economic, and studies with regard to alternative techniques for power supply at individual locations. Overall studies of energy and coal requirements and supplies have been conducted and in addition data on individual projects have been utilized.

High-speed diesel oil is used by the truck industry. As stated earlier, motor spirit is consumed by trucks only to a negligible extent. The growth in the number of trucks on the road has been projected by taking the existing stock, allowing for additions resulting from domestic production and deducting the number of vehicles likely to be scrapped. Allowance has been made also for increased intensity in the use of trucks, and higher consumption of fuel per mile as a result of a shift towards heavier trucks and growing use of trailers.

While initial estimates have been made on the basis of the given production plans for trucks, studies are also being undertaken of the relative roles of road and rail transport. To an extent, the two are complementary. Increasingly, however, long-distance goods haulage, particularly of high value items is being taken over from the railways by trucks. Improvement of highways has accentuated this trend. The question arises whether such a shift is economic if it involves under-utilization of rail capacity which has already been installed. In so far as additional investments are needed in any case a choice has to be made between rail and road movement. The higher foreign exchange cost of road as compared to rail transport would be relevant; railways on the other hand are more capital intensive. Shadow prices for capital and foreign exchange are among the relevant techniques for comparison of alternatives.

Low-speed diesel oil is used for agricultural pumps, stationary diesel engines for industry, etc. Estimates of consumption are based on production forecasts for the relevant types of engines, which in turn are related, as far as agricultural pumps are concerned, to the agricultural development programme.

Kerosene is used for lighting purposes in areas in which electricity is not available, and as a cooking fuel. Demand estimates have been based on past trends, with allowance being made for higher projected rate of income growth in the rural areas and for rural electrification. A distinction has been drawn between superior kerosene used in relatively sophisticated lamps and inferior kerosene which is capable of being used only to secure an open flame. Inferior kerosene enters into the consumption of the lowest income groups only. Another demand for kerosene is as fuel for jet engines, and this requirement has been projected on the basis of the anticipated growth rate of air transport.

The growth rate of consumption of lubricants is anticipated to correspond roughly to that of output in manufacturing industries.

Furnace oil can be used directly as an industrial fuel, as a substitute for coal or power. The studies of energy and coal requirements referred to earlier provided a basis for projecting these requirements.

Production estimates for the various categories of petroleum products have been based on the refining programme, which in turn allows both for use of indigenous and of imported crude. There are technical limits to the proportion of kerosene and diesel oil, as opposed to motor-spirit which can be extracted from crude, and comparison of likely production with demand reveals, for the next few years, surpluses of motor-spirit and deficits of diesel oil and kerosene. In due course, however, expansion of naphtha-based industries is expected to result in absorption of all available naphtha supplies. In the meanwhile, account has been taken of motor-spirit surpluses in the export programme.

The pricing of petroleum products is very relevant to demand projections and presents complicated problems. It is considered desirable to keep kerosene prices relatively low as this commodity is consumed by lower income groups. Similarly, the price of low-speed diesel oil is kept relatively low because it is an input of agriculture. To an extent, however, kerosene and low-speed diesel oil are capable of admixture with high-speed diesel oil as a fuel for motor vehicles. This sets limits to the price of high-speed diesel oil and thus to the possibility of substituting surplus motor-spirit for scarce high-speed diesel oil in motor-vehicle consumption through shifts in relative prices. Both kerosene and diesel prices have, however, been raised in the recent past with a noticeable impact on consumption of kerosene, though not on that of high-speed diesel oil as the degree of shift necessary to induce substitution of motor-spirit for high-speed diesel is considerable. The increased availability of coal as a result of larger production in the recent past may be expected also to have an impact on the relative consumption of coal and furnace oil. In this whole area, demand projections require frequent revision in the light of policy induced and autonomous changes in relative prices and decisions with regard to investment programmes. From the point of view of foreign exchange budgeting, changes in world prices must also be taken into account. The weakness in the world oil market in the recent past has meant that outlays to secure given quantities of supplies can be reduced.

Foodgrains

We now turn to the estimation of demand for foodgrains. The basic approach has been to consider the effect of increases in income and of changes in pattern of consumption associated with urbanization.

173

Other factors such as the age composition of population, family size and income distribution were assumed to remain constant for want of adequate information. Constant prices were assumed.

In one study of the demand for foodgrains, the last year of the Second Five Year Plan, 1960–1, was taken as the base year. The supply in the base year was calculated from production data adjusted for exports, imports and, where possible, for changes in stocks. The estimated requirements for intermediate uses (for example, seed) were deducted initially from the total internal supply to obtain the quantities used for final personal consumption. The consumption of each foodgrain was distributed between rural and urban areas in the same proportion as their respective aggregate expenditures on that foodgrain. Expenditure distribution between rural and urban areas was worked out on the basis of census estimates of rural and urban population and *per capita* expenditures derived from National Sample Survey Studies. Future demand was projected on alternative assumptions regarding the growth rate of the economy and the proportion of income devoted to private consumption. Population projections were based on census data and some acceleration of the rate of urbanization was allowed for. Rural and urban elasticities of demand at constant prices relative to *per capita* consumption expenditute were worked out on the basis of National Sample Survey data. These were then applied to the income and population projections to derive the growth in urban and rural demand for foodgrains. Allowances for seed, feed, wastage, etc. were then added back on the basis of available data regarding past consumption for these purposes.

Further work being done includes testing of the stability and statistical significance of elasticities on the basis of cross-section data for different points of time, pooling of time series and cross-section data for estimating the effect of price changes on consumption, examination of cross-section data with a view to finding out whether there is any significant difference in pattern of consumption for comparable levels of income between different occupations and between families of different sizes and age composition, and study of demand patterns with special reference to regional peculiarities in regard to food-grains.

The estimation of food production as a result of the agricultural development programme has been based on technical ratios relating additional inputs of fertilizers etc. to additional outputs. These have been derived from a number of farm studies and experimental data. There are obvious statistical difficulties in estimating the specific contribution made to output by additional supplies of any single input; the additional output resulting from more intensive application of fertilizers would depend, for example, on the intensity of irrigation.

The assumption of constant prices has also not held in reality. There have been policy induced increases in prices in order to secure an adequate return to the farmer and to stimulate production. There have further been periods of shortages during which prices have risen well beyond the levels considered desirable from the long run point of view. Supplies of foodgrains have been made in urban areas, however, at relatively constant prices from imported stocks and stocks of domestic produce procured by the Government. Statistical evidence regarding the impact of higher prices on aggregate consumption is at present scanty. Urban consumers and agricultural labourers with wages fixed at least partly in money terms may be expected to react to higher prices by consuming less. On the other hand, farmers with a marketable surplus may to an extent increase consumption of their own produce when the prices of food production rise relative to those of manufactures. Shifts in distribution channels as a result of regulatory measures make estimation of the true impact of price changes on marketable surplus difficult. Meanwhile, short run estimates have to be made of import requirements to hold prices in urban areas and to build up a minimum level of stocks under Government control.

Imports of foodgrains are substantially under the American Public Law—480 programme. Under this programme, however, certain normal purchases are required to be made by the recipient country from its own resources. Further, freight charges at world freight rates have to be paid in convertible currency by the recipient country. Estimated payments for imports have thus to be broken up into payments in foreign exchange and payments in local currency.

Other Commodities

Fairly detailed estimates of import requirements are made also for certain other importsnt commodities such as non-ferrous metals, raw cotton, drugs and machinery. For miscellaneous items however, less detailed methods have to be employed. In the case of finished consumer goods, it is assumed that, broadly, the current levels of imports will continue—demand being restricted through quantitative restrictions or duties, Imports of miscellaneous metal products are also assumed to remain constant in view of the import substitution programme for engineering goods. While such short cuts are necesssry and inevitable when formulating the medium-term programme, detailed consideration of indivudal items is naturally necessary in preparing short run programmes.

III. CHANNELS OF COMMUNICATION REQUIRED FOR FORMULATION OF A FOREIGN TRADE PLAN

The preparation of a detailed foreign trade plan involves in effect projections of all important economic variables, in a fair degree of detail. The watching of the progress under the Plan and its periodic revision again requires reassessment of the past progress and medium term prospects of the entire economy. The authorities engaged in the preparation and up-dating of the medium-term foreign trade plan have thus not only to rely on foreign trade and balance-of-payments data but also to secure a steady flow of information from other authorities concerned with production and investment plans. The watching of progress and revision of forecasts will throw up policy problems which then have to be taken up with the authorities concerned with taxation, price regulation, production planning, etc.

The first elementary step is to compare actual performance with regard to imports and exports with the forecast made earlier. For this purpose, commodity-wise foreign trade statistics and payments and receipts data maintained by the Central Bank would have to be utilized. When there is import licensing and exchange control, statistics regarding issue of import licences and release of foreign exchange will, when compared with data on actual payments and imports, provide the basis for short-term forecasting. Statistics of agricultural and industrial production, as reported by the statistical authorities collecting such data, can be used to check the extent to which production assumptions have been fulfilled. Adjustment for imports and exports will indicate the variations of actual consumption from anticipated levels. Price data which may be collected both for construction of price indices and as an administrative by-product of the work of the agricultural, industrial and other departments must flow into the office concerned with forecasting, so that the impact on prices of any divergences between anticipated and actual supply levels can be noted.

Revision of forward estimates in the light of past experience calls for up-dating of estimates for future years of demand and production varying the price assumptions, if necessary. The authorities looking after production in different sectors would have to provide a continuing flow of information with regard to revision of forward estimates of outputs over the period of the medium-term Plan. The basis of revisions—e.g. delay in preparation of project reports, delay in negotiating external assistance for financing project imports, etc.— must be specified, to facilitate checking. Such estimates would also have to specify the extent to which the inputs used will be indigenous and imported respectively, and the supply of indigenous inputs allowed for will have to be checked against independent estimates of the production of these items. For example, the estimates of output of engineering industries will involve certain assumptions regarding the consumption of domestic and imported steel; the availability of indigenous steel at the level assumed will have to be checked with reference to the forecasts of the managers of the major steel plants. Initially, allowance will have to be made for import of the steel supplies required by engineering industry to meet demand at current prices, given a certain availability of steel from local production. If aggregation shows that the overall picture that emerges is not a tenable one, having regard to the likely availability of foreign exchange from exports and foreign capital inflow, thought will have to be given to the reformulation of the foreign trade plan to restore balance.

An important part of the exercise will consist in projecting the increases in industrial capacities likely in the next three or four years from investment decisions already taken and the implications of these for output and trade balance. There will be relatively little room for manœuvre with regard to such additions to capacity except of course that, in the short run, it may be necessary to put up with temporary under-utilization of industrial capacity if no other course of action is available. The review may, however, throw up guide-lines with regard to further investment decisions in order to restore external balance with optimal use of the production capacity within the country.

Demand estimates based on income growth, levels of investment etc. can be reviewed by the forecasting agency itself on the basis of the revised projections based on recent past experience. The agency will be able to throw up suggestions as to the direction and possible magnitude of the adjustment needed in the macro-economic variables, such as the level of public investment, disposable private incomes and direct public sector outlays on imports which appear to be necessary from the point of view of a balanced foreign trade plan.

The medium run is a succession of short runs and those concerned with the medium-term Plan have to work in close co-operation with the officials handling short-term foreign exchange budgeting. It is easy in short-term planning to relieve immediate pressures while sacrificing the requirements of medium- and long-term balance. There is also often a temptation in short term budgeting to make only marginal changes or to make broadly equal adjustments for all items. Sensible short-term decisions can only be taken if the implications for the medium- and long-term growth of the economy are kept constantly in mind.